Still • Falling

The Code

T0007284

Still • Falling

The Code

Two Plays for Teens

Study Guides included

Rachel Aberle

with a foreword by Joan MacLeod

Talonbooks

© 2022 Rachel Aberle
Foreword © 2022 Joan MacLeod
Study Guides © 2022 Green Thumb Theatre

All rights reserved. No part of this book may be reproduced, stored in a
retrieval system, or transmitted, in any form or by any means, without the
prior written consent of the publisher or a licence from Access Copyright
(the Canadian Copyright Licensing Agency). For a copyright licence, visit
accesscopyright.ca or call toll-free 1-800-893-5777.

Talonbooks
9259 Shaughnessy Street, Vancouver, British Columbia, Canada V6P 6R4
talonbooks.com

Talonbooks is located on xʷməθkʷəy̓əm, Sk̲wx̲wú7mesh, and səlilwətaʔɬ Lands.

First printing: 2022

Typeset in Minion
Printed and bound in Canada on 100% post-consumer recycled paper
Interior and cover design by Typesmith
Cover illustration by Ginger Sedlarova

Talonbooks acknowledges the financial support of the Canada Council for
the Arts, the Government of Canada through the Canada Book Fund, and the
Province of British Columbia through the British Columbia Arts Council and
the Book Publishing Tax Credit.

Rachel Aberle acknowledges the support of Green Thumb Theatre and the
Banff Centre for Arts and Creativity.

Rights to produce *Still • Falling* and *The Code*, in whole or in part, in any
medium by any group, amateur or professional, are retained by the author.
Interested persons are requested to contact Talonbooks at 9259 Shaughnessy
Street, Vancouver, British Columbia, Canada, V6P 6R4; telephone (toll-free):
1-888-445-4176; email: info@talonbooks.com; website: talonbooks.com.

Library and Archives Canada Cataloguing in Publication

Title: Still--falling ; The code : two plays for teens / Rachel Aberle.
Other titles: Plays. Works | Code
Names: Aberle, Rachel, author. | Container of (work): Aberle, Rachel. Still--
falling | Container of (work): Aberle, Rachel. Code
Identifiers: Canadiana 20210327278 | ISBN 9781772013993 (softcover)
Classification: LCC PS8601.B455 A6 2022 | DDC C812/.6—DC23

Please note: These plays deal with difficult subject matter, including anxiety, depression, non-suicidal self-harm, gendered harassment, and bullying.

To Elliot, who is still too young
for these plays, but whom I
love with my whole being

Foreword

There's nothing quite like starting the day by watching a play at nine thirty in the morning in a room filled with teenagers. They can be a tough crowd – letting you know if they're bored or sleepy or more interested in who's sitting behind them than what's happening on stage. But if they're engaged – as they were from the first to the final line of the production of *Still • Falling* I saw in a high school in Victoria – well, that's a beautiful thing. The remarkable Olivia Hutt played the role of Nina and also gave voice to several other characters in this one-person show about anxiety and depression – Mom, Dad, little brother, friends at school, and her therapist. Watching with an audience of young women, I saw how strongly they connected with this first play by Rachel Aberle. The dialogue was distinct and vivid. It always rang true and sometimes was really funny. When roped into joining the Drama Club, for example, Nina says, "I'm not an actor! I mean, I took creative writing ... It's basically the opposite ... The 'Standing Around Awkwardly club' had an epic waitlist."

But it's Nina's internal voice that breaks our hearts: "I'm thinking about how ever since I got up this morning, my skin didn't feel like it fit." This intelligent and gifted fifteen-year-old is so hard on herself even when she is succeeding in making friends at her new school: "I know I sound like an idiot, okay?" When a popular male student is interested in her, she doesn't trust what he says and imagines what he sees: "He can see everything I've been trying to hide. I know it."

How to be fifteen and escape misery? I'm not sure. Without question what is happening to Nina – or, indeed, Nick in the second version of this script – is much more serious than teenage angst. But there is comfort in hearing from characters like Nina and Nick. Others suffer, too. All of us do. We're human.

In some ways, Moira in *The Code* is a polar opposite of Nina. Moira is confident, not afraid of confrontation, and has a keen sense of justice. She's very good friends with two other students – Connor, a "slacker and wannabe ladies' man," and Simon, who is "hopelessly smitten with Moira." The play is set in an outdoor hangout outside their school. And these three feel like outsiders. There is something about that status that makes us invested in this trio right from the start. Again the dialogue is vivid, layered with their long history of friendship, and it's often funny. But friendship is also a complicated business – especially when Simon misreads what he was hoping was romantic interest from Moira. He feels rejected, so he strikes back. Messy, human stuff.

The plot of *The Code* has many turns and twists I hadn't seen coming but are beautifully set up. Rachel Aberle's storytelling skills are first-rate here. In the end, *The Code* shows us how social media, public shaming, and distorting the truth can devastate. At its heart, this is a play about consent and the importance of friendship. I would give anything to watch a production of it with a group of students – first thing in the morning or anytime, anywhere.

—JOAN MACLEOD
Playwright, Victoria, BC

Playwright's Note

I have been asked more than a few times why I write for teen audiences. More interesting than any reason I could come up with is why people ask that question in the first place. Why shouldn't I write for teens? Teens are human beings with complex lives and struggles that are worth exploring. From a writer's standpoint, they have the advantage of facing some of these issues for the very first time. What could be more interesting?

After the "why" often comes the "how." How do I write for teens? Do I hang out at high-school bus stops to eavesdrop? Do I scour TikTok (or whatever social media platform is at its peak) searching for the latest lingo? No. In fact I have found my attempts to remain "current" have usually backfired. Just ask the first cast of *The Code*, who had to hold for laughs every time Simon uttered the line "Winter formal was lit." The line was not supposed to be a joke.

Writing for teens requires adaptability. Both *Still • Falling* and *The Code* have changed since their initial productions in order to stay up to date. They may change again after this publication for the same reasons. I will always be open to discussing how these plays can best serve their intended audiences. As Green Thumb Theatre was preparing to produce a live-streamed digital adaptation of their production of *Still • Falling* in the spring of 2021, after touring the show live for four consecutive seasons, I decided the play needed more than just an update to provide a platform for discussion about mental health to as many teens as possible. I set about adapting the script to explore the story through the eyes of a teenage boy, and so a new adaptation, following Nick instead of Nina, came into existence.

To answer both the "how" and "why" questions as best I can: I write for teens by writing for myself. Somehow adults forget that the issues we deal with are the same issues young people are facing. Perhaps they see them through a slightly different lens, but they are not living in an alternate reality dominated by "teen issues." I started experiencing depression in my teens and have experienced anxiety for as long as I can remember. I started noticing everyday sexism and gendered harassment in my teens, and unfortunately it is of course a part of my life to this day. So I wrote plays about those things.

I hope you like them.

—RACHEL ABERLE

Still • Falling

(Nina)

PRODUCTION HISTORY

Still • Falling (Nina) was first produced in the fall of 2015 by Green Thumb Theatre in Vancouver, British Columbia, with the following cast and crew:

NINA	Olivia Hutt
Director	Patrick McDonald
Stage Manager	Heather Thompson
Apprentice Stage Manager	Geoff Jones
Set Designer	Ken MacDonald
Projection Designer	Cameron Fraser
Props and Costume Buyer	Tina Ozols

CHARACTERS

NINA, a fifteen-year-old girl. By all outward appearances, she is absolutely "typical." She moves between speaking to the audience, speaking in real time to her therapist, and reliving her story. As she moves through her memories, she moves about her therapist's office space; when she is speaking to her therapist, she returns to her chair. At times she speaks as the other characters in her life, indicated by the character's name in parentheses before the line.

SETTING

The play takes place in Nina's therapist's office. Throughout the play, projections and audio may be used to indicate location changes associated with Nina's memories.

NINA sits in her therapist's office. She takes in her surroundings and then looks across at where her therapist would be sitting. She glances at a clock.

NINA

10:05 a.m. We were supposed to start five minutes ago. It's Tuesday morning and I'm supposed to be in school. There are so many things about being here that feel weird, but that's probably the weirdest. School is pretty much top priority in my family, like... We're the kind of people that schedule dentist appointments at 7 a.m. so that we can fit it in before the first bell.

The door swings open and she swoops in. When you hear the word "therapist," there's, like, specific things you think of, right? Y'know... Sigmund Freud... suspenders and really bushy eyebrows. This woman has perfect hair, perfect nails, and a perfectly coordinated outfit. My therapist. Brought to you by L'Oréal / Ralph Lauren (*the brand name may be changed to reflect current trends*).

She arranges herself in the armchair across from me, smoothes her pale-pink skirt, opens her notebook, clicks her pen, and says, "Good morning."

(*to the therapist*) Hi. I mean, good morning. Um... nice office. I mean, I guess it's nice. What do I know?

(*narrating*) I know I sound like an idiot, okay? "Nice office?" What am I even talking about? God, thirty seconds in and I'm already doing this wrong.

(*to the therapist*) Pardon me? When did I get here? Um... like... ten minutes ago? Your receptionist let me in – oh! To Vancouver? Grade ten. I mean, a week and a half before grade ten started. It was a Tuesday night, taco night.

TRANSITION to the dinner table. NINA indicates her
    family members as she describes them.

The Professor (that's my dad) is at his spot at this end of
the table, his nose buried deep in what has got to be one of
the world's most boring books, seriously. He's a professor
of economics – which he *actually* thinks is interesting –
so basically, unless you want to talk about dollars and
cents and, like, I don't know... yen... good luck getting his
attention.

Over here we have Little Miss Sunshine, the creator of Taco
Tuesdays, Beef Wellington Wednesdays, and Family Night
Fridays – ladies and gentlemen, Suzanne Walker, my mother.
She's, like, the polar opposite of my dad. He's on another
planet and she is RIGHT HERE, IN YOUR FACE, asking,
"How was your day? Would you like a mini quiche?" She's...
the life of the party. Even when there is no party.

And right here is my little brother Tyler... the Creep. I'm
convinced he's an eight-year-old troll/human hybrid my
parents found under a bridge.

(*as the Creep*) I am not a troll.

(*as herself, like she's caught him*) Spoken like a true troll!

Then there's me, right here – Nina Walker.

So here we are, halfway through the summer before I start
grade ten, tacos assembled, ready to dive in when suddenly –

(*as Little Miss Sunshine*) Attention, kiddios –

(*as herself, narrating*) I hate when she calls us that.

(*as Little Miss Sunshine*) Your dad and I have some exciting
    news. Honey – do you want to tell them?

(*as herself, narrating*) The Professor looks up from his book and focuses on the three of us. It's like we've materialized from nothing and he has no idea who we are.

(*as Little Miss Sunshine*) Honey, I was telling the kids we have news. You want to tell them your exciting announcement?

(*as the Professor*) Uh… right. News. Yes… announcement! We are moving. To Vancouver. In a month.

(*as herself, narrating*) WHAT?!

(*as the Creep*) Yes! British Columbia is home to the *Ariolimax columbianus*!

(*as herself, to the Creep*) What are you talking about?

(*as the Creep*) The Pacific banana slug! Fact! If you lick them, your tongue goes numb!

(*as herself, to the Creep*) What?

(*as the Creep*) Maybe I'll get to lick one!

(*as herself, to Little Miss Sunshine*) Mom! What am I supposed to do? Y'know… friends, school? My life?!

(*as Little Miss Sunshine*) I know. Nina, I know it might seem like you're going to be giving up a lot. But think about what you'll be gaining. You are going to make so many new friends and try so many new things. We can go skiing! Watch the whales! And the school has a specialized creative-writing program. Your life is going to be filled right up with good things. Everything is going to be fine, Nina – better than fine! You are going to *love* Vancouver.

TRANSITION *to NINA standing in front of her new school, looking up at it.*

Vancouver is grey and wet, and the school... the school is huge. Everyone around me knows where they're going and knows each other. I don't know anything. What was Little Miss Sunshine thinking? I don't belong here.

I go to walk into the school. My legs have turned to lead. My heart feels like it's going to burst through my chest. I want to go home, I want to disappear. I want to do anything but walk into this building.

(*giving herself a pep talk*) Think of something good, some Good Things. Relax. I can't relax! I can't even breathe!

Suddenly this girl grabs me by the elbow –

(*as Kate, yelling*) What are you doing? Come inside, you're soaking wet!

(*as herself, narrating*) She pulls me through the front door. Once we're inside, she collapses her umbrella, looks at me from head to toe, and starts laughing.

(*as Kate*) You must be some kind of crazy. What were you doing? You were like a statue out there.

(*as herself, to Kate*) It's my first day. I don't really know where I'm going.

(*as Kate*) 'Kay, well, the office is that way. What's your name?

(*as herself, to Kate*) Nina.

(*as Kate*) Cool. See ya.

(*as herself, narrating*) I don't even get her name before she disappears.

The first two classes go okay. I make it through without getting lost or – more importantly – turning into a statue again. At lunch I walk into the cafeteria. It's massive. Then I start to feel it again – the pounding heart, the shallow breath.

(*as Kate*) Tina! You're alive! How were your first couple classes?

(*as herself, narrating*) It's the girl from the beginning of the day. It takes me a second to understand that she's talking to me.

(*as Kate*) Tina! Tina! Earth to Tina! How's it going?

(*as herself, to Kate*) What? Oh. Hi. Nina. It's Nina.

(*as Kate*) Right, sorry, my bad. Come sit with us! We are totally nice. We hardly ever bite.

(*as herself, narrating*) She still hasn't told me her name, but it doesn't take long to figure out. Everybody knows this girl. Kate Sidhu. Empress of the Third Table from the Door. People come by and say hi, sit with us for a bit, then move along when someone else comes along that she'd rather talk to. Somehow I make the cut every time. A few minutes into lunch, a blond girl with fake nails and super-long eyelashes shows up and Kate dismisses a couple of people to make space.

(*as Kate*) Nina, this is Ash. Ash, Nina.

(*as Ash*) Hi Nina. I'm Kate's soulmate and sister from another mister.

(*as Kate*) Ash, this is Nina's first day. I found her frozen like a statue outside the school before first bell and it was the cutest thing I've ever seen. We're adopting her.

TRANSITION to the dinner table.

(*as Little Miss Sunshine*) Attention, Walker family, attention, please! Everyone, raise a glass! A toast to our very first Vancouver Mix-and-Match Monday!

(*as herself, narrating*) Mix-and-Match Monday has always been Little Miss Sunshine's favourite dinner theme. We're all responsible for making one of the items for dinner. The Creep boiled water – which shouldn't count, OBVIOUSLY, but he gets away with *everything* – I made a salad, Little Miss Sunshine made handmade chicken-and-pesto ravioli with homemade sun-dried tomato sauce, and the Professor made his specialty: Oreos®. Double Stuf®.

(*as Little Miss Sunshine*) So! Let's hear it! Worsts and bests! I want a full report!

(*as herself, narrating*) This is another one of Little Miss Sunshine's favourite things. At dinner we all have to share the worst thing that happened to us that day and the best.

(*as Little Miss Sunshine*) All right Nina, take it away...

(*as herself, narrating*) I start to answer, but when I try to think of a "worst"... all I can think of is being stuck in front of the school... (*breathing unevenly*) I can't talk about this.

(*as herself, to her family*) Um... If you don't ask Dad soon, you'll lose him into whatever book he's reading.

(*as Little Miss Sunshine*) Gordon, put your book down! Give us a worst and a best!

(*as the Professor*) Of course. Worsts and bests. Worst... unbelievable. I learned today that one of my fourth-year advanced classes – ADVANCED CLASSES – doesn't know the first thing about the restructuring of the Brazilian monetary system in 1994. So, needless to say, they are woefully behind! Best... ah! The coffee shop down the block makes a perfect espresso. (*returning to his book*) It. Is. Perfect.

(*as the Creep*) I'll go next! Best part: easy. Found a slug after school and I brought it home. Worst part? Now I can't find him.

(*as herself, narrating*) I look over at Little Miss Sunshine. Slug lost somewhere in the house? This is when an ordinary mom would flip out. Instead, Little Miss Sunshine says:

(*as Little Miss Sunshine*) So... family slug hunt after dinner! Great! All right Nina, back to you. Worst and best, what happened today?

(*as herself, to Little Miss Sunshine*) Um... I don't know. I didn't have a "worst."

(*as Little Miss Sunshine*) Excellent! And? Best?

(*as herself, to Little Miss Sunshine*) I guess... I mean, I think I... made some friends?

TRANSITION to school as NINA says the following lines.

Becoming friends with Kate is, like, a crazy-lucky break. It's basically like having an answer key to everything about this school. You name it – she knows it. Where to sit, who to talk to, what to wear – and for whatever reason, she feels like sharing it all with me.

(*as Kate, talking about other people in the hallway as they pass by*) That's Krista DeWitt. I know, she doesn't look real, right? It's like someone used a reverse shrink ray on a Barbie doll. Get this – earlier in the year, we were learning about, like, King Arthur and Merlin in English, and she ACTUALLY asked if dragons were extinct. Actually. That's Marissa

Choi – she has two older brothers and her parents go out of town ALL the time, so we'll definitely go to parties at her house. She's cool. Oh, and that – okay, put your eyes back in your head. That's Ian Nakamura. I know, right? Hot. He's in grade eleven, super, super, super funny guy.

(*as herself, narrating*) So as much as I make fun of Little Miss Sunshine for her motivational speeches and overall cheerleader attitude, maybe she was right.

In October, me, Kate, and Ash all go to the Halloween dance together, dressed as the Three Blind Mice. We're all wearing sunglasses, which Ash refuses to take off.

(*as Ash*) Come on guys, they're integral to the character. Without them, we're just mice.

(*as herself, narrating*) Only problem is, the lights in the gym are really dark, so she keeps bumping into everything. At the end of the night, she locks eyes with Tom Brockton, who she's been obsessed with for, like, forever. She heads over to ask him to dance, but because she can't see anything she trips over Amir Nazari's dragon tail, knocking into the speaker system, which topples over *directly* on Tom – who breaks his ankle. Needless to say, he doesn't speak to Ash for the rest of the term.

Oh! And creative writing. The class is really cool, and we put out a newspaper for the whole school every month. In December, one of my short stories gets picked to be in the paper, and when Kate reads it, she acts like I deserve a Nobel Prize or something.

(*as Kate*) Um, what the hell, Nina? You didn't tell me you were, like... Shakespeare or whatever!

(*as Ash*) Who?

(*as Kate*) Shakespeare.

>*Beat.*

Like… Shakespeare? William Shakespeare.

(*as Ash*) Saying the name over and over doesn't make me know who it is.

(*as Kate, to Ash*) You are hopeless. (*to NINA*) Anyway – your story. Good! Really, really good. I can't believe you kept your genius a secret this long. I don't know if I can forgive you!

(*as herself, narrating*) By Christmas break I'm feeling really solid. I like this city, I like my friends, and I like my school. Good Things.

TRANSITION to Nina's bedroom.

(*as Little Miss Sunshine, calling from outside Nina's bedroom door*) Nina! Hello! Wakey-wakey, eggs and bakey! Just kidding, there's only cereal. Come on! Get up! It's Christmas-Tree Day!

(*as herself, narrating*) It's December twenty-third: Christmas-Tree Day, another important day in Walker Family Tradition. We all go out two days before Christmas, pick out a tree, bring it home, and decorate it. The only rule is we have to pick out the saddest, rattiest, Charlie-Browniest tree possible, and make it beautiful. I know… It sounds totally corny… but it's fun.

I open my closet and stand there.

Jeans or skirt? Jeans or skirt? Jeans or skirt? This isn't rocket science, what's wrong with me? Jeans or skirt?

I can't breathe. My skin feels all cold and… I have tears in my eyes.

NINA turns from the closet and goes to write in her journal.

Normal girl

Normal heart

Normal brain

Then it starts

A creeping feeling: sorrow, dread

A tiny voice inside my head

Stay inside, keep out of sight

Something in you isn't right

Venom in you, dark as night

Ugly, shameful, full of spite

Frightened girl

Jagged heart

Crooked mind

Tears you apart

Horrid girl

Broken brain

Ugly heart

Am I insane?

NINA closes her journal, puts it away, and TRANSITIONS into sitting once again in the therapist's office.

The therapist sits, scratching away on her notepad. She's been that way since the moment I started talking. Now that I've stopped for a second, she looks up at me, totally unfazed. I don't know what I expected... some kind of reaction, I guess? A raised eyebrow, maybe? But she just looks back at me silently, waiting for me to continue.

(*to the therapist*) So, I mean... that's totally weird, right?

(*as herself, narrating*) She shrugs her shoulders, like she for real has no opinion on the matter. I do not get this woman. She's so freakin'... calm and collected, I might as well be listing off my top ten favourite foods, or describing a really mediocre sunset I saw one time.

(*to the therapist*) Pardon? Do *I* think it's weird? Well, like, obviously, or I wouldn't have asked you. Aren't you supposed to be telling me what's weird and what's normal and, like... what's wrong with me? (*pause as the therapist asks a question*) Well, if I didn't think there was something wrong with me, I wouldn't be here! Isn't that, like, completely obvious? (*pause*) I'm *not* mad, I'm just... whatever. What do you want me to talk about now? Keep going? Fine.

TRANSITION to the family living room.

It's Christmas morning and we're opening gifts.

(*as Little Miss Sunshine*) Is there something you want to say to your brother?

(*as herself, narrating*) I know where I am, but I have no idea what Little Miss Sunshine is talking about.

(*as herself, to Little Miss Sunshine*) Huh?

(*as Little Miss Sunshine*) You've been raised to say "thank you" when someone gives you a gift, Nina.

(*as herself, to Little Miss Sunshine*) What?

(*as herself, narrating*) I look down at my hand. I'm holding a solid-brass banana slug. Life-sized. I look across the living room and the Creep is sitting there, eyes brimming with tears, looking totally defeated.

(*as the Creep*) It's a paperweight. Cuz you like writing. I thought you would like it.

(*as herself, narrating*) I remember opening the thing. I remember thinking, "Say thank you now." But instead I just sat there, staring at the floor. Time stopped. I look up at the Creep.

(*as herself, to the Creep*) I do, man. It's totally awesome. Thank you. For real.

TRANSITION *back to school as* **NINA** *delivers the following lines.*

January fifth comes. Finally. Christmas break is supposed to be fun, relaxing, but I just felt like... sometimes I was on another planet. Other times, it was like I was drowning.

It's okay. I just have to stop being such a freak. I know getting back to school will fix this. I'll see my friends, I'll have stuff to do. Both Good Things.

My relief evaporates when Kate announces:

(*as Kate*) You, me, and Ash are all joining drama club.

(*as herself, narrating*) Ash chimes in –

(*as Ash*) Acting, bitchez!

NINA stands, frozen for a moment, visibly stressed.

(*as Kate*) Hello, Nina. What's wrong with you? Why do you look like I just told you we're joining a spider-eating club?

(*as herself, to Kate*) I – I'm not an actor! I mean, I took creative writing… It's basically the opposite. We don't stand up in front of people talking, we sit in corners and write all by ourselves.

(*as Kate*) Okay, take a breath, Shakespeare. Don't worry! You're not going to act, you're going to write stuff for me and Ash. You'll be our secret weapon!

(*as herself, narrating*) And before I know it, we're in the drama room. Because it's the first meeting, we have to go around the room and say why we're here. People say things like:

(*as Chivaun*) Hey, I'm Chivaun… grade ten. I've just, like… always really respected what acting is about, you know? Like… seeing the world through another person's eyes? I feel like if everyone could do that, the world would be, like, such a better place. Namaste.

(*as herself, narrating*) Everyone's taking it super seriously. Well… almost everyone.

(*as Ash*) I'm Ash. Saggitarius. Are we going to have to kiss for any of the scenes? Like, it's fine if we do. Like, I'm fine with that. Like, if you give me a scene with kissing? That's totally fine. That's just, like… acting, y'know?

(*as herself, narrating*) And then it's my turn.

(*as herself, to her class*) Hi.

Beat.

I'm Nina.

Beat.

Um, I'm not really into acting.

Beat.

So obviously, drama club was the natural choice.

Beat.

The "Standing Around Awkwardly club" had an epic waitlist.

I'm ready for a room of blank stares, but instead,
people laugh.

(*as herself, to her class*) Okay. So I'll make you guys a deal. I'll
write skits for you guys to perform as long as you *never* make
me talk in front of a group again. Fair?

(*as herself, narrating*) This guy across the circle from me
gives me a huge smile. It's super-hilarious, super-hot Ian
Nakamura, who's in grade eleven. Smiling. At me.

Every meeting we have after that, I make sure that I have
some skits ready and... it never fails. Every meeting, people
want to hear my stuff. They all laugh when I hoped they
would laugh, and almost always someone comes up to me
afterwards to say, "good job." It feels... incredible.

*TRANSITION to the bathroom. NINA is hiding, breathing
unevenly, trying not to break down sobbing.*

I'm in the last stall in the bathroom on the third floor, at the
far end of the hall. The one with the chipped paint around
the lock and the graffiti that says "Shannon is a bitch" next
to "Grad 2017." I'm here because nobody ever comes into this
bathroom. I'm here because I'm... I'm losing my mind.

What is wrong with me? Everything's been great since school started back up, since I can see my friends again, since things have been going well in drama club, but today, it's just like Christmas break. Today...

I didn't want to come to school today. The moment my eyes opened today, I knew that I needed to stay home. I TOLD Little Miss Sunshine that I wasn't feeling well, but she took my temperature and when it was fine, she told me to "buck up."

NINA takes a moment to compose herself.

I come out of the stall and I look in the mirror.

That's when I see it. What everyone else must see. Me. Total loser panic-stricken freak. Bad. And ugly. Bad and ugly. Bad... ugly!

NINA slaps herself in the face. It shocks her.

(*slapping*) Bad! (*slapping*) Ugly!

NINA breathes heavily, working to regain her composure.

TRANSITION to the therapist's office. NINA responds to questions from the therapist.

I wouldn't call it "hiding out." It's a bathroom... It's a public place. I just go there to... take a break.

Beat.

I don't know! A break from everything, I guess.

Beat.

No, that's the point, I don't know why I needed a break…
I never know why. This is so stupid. I'm sorry. It didn't
happen a lot, okay? At first it was just now and then.

TRANSITION back to school. NINA is at her locker.

After drama club one day, I feel a tap on my shoulder. It's Ian
Nakamura.

(*as Ian*) Nina, what's up? I liked what you wrote today.
You're funny.

(*as herself, to Ian*) Thanks.

(*as Ian*) So you wanna write something brilliant for me?
We could work on it together.

(*as herself, narrating*) I don't know what to say. Or, I mean,
I do – YES! YES, LET'S TOTALLY DO THAT! But it's like
I'm frozen to the spot, the words just won't come. Ian starts
to turn to go.

(*as Ian*) Okay, never mind, no sweat…

(*as herself, to Ian, shouting*) Wait! (*at a normal level, trying to
regain her cool*) Um, I mean… hold up.

(*as Ian*) I was starting to think you might be a mime.

(*as herself, to Ian*) Yes! Yes. I mean, no! I'm not a mime. But um,
yes. We should totally work on scenes together.

(*as Ian*) Cool. Want to meet up today after school? I'll pick you
up. I mean not literally… that would be weird, right? If I, like,
picked you up and carried you out of the school? But, like,
I'll come to your locker and then we'll both walk in the same
direction at the same time… sound good?

(*as herself, narrating*) Ian is… really nice. That first afternoon
we go to this coffee shop near school and talk about scenes I
could write for him. I'm taking notes on everything we talk
about, but after about an hour, Ian reaches over and closes
my binder.

(*as Ian*) Okay, I have a confession. I had a selfish reason for
wanting to hang out with you today.

(*as herself, to Ian*) Isn't hanging out with me so I'll write scenes
for you already selfish?

(*as Ian, laughing*) Okay, so I'm just selfish all around –
everyone's got flaws, right? Look, I think you're interesting.
Like… who are you? I feel like you have a secret identity.

(*as herself, narrating*) When he says this, he looks me right
in the eye, like he's looking for something. Looking for
my secrets. And just like that, I'm not in the coffee shop
anymore. I'm in the bathroom on the third floor again,
hiding out, hitting myself in the face. Freak! I am such a
freak, and he knows. He can see everything I've been trying
to hide. I know it.

(*as Ian*) So, are you going to be around this weekend?

(*as herself, narrating*) I ask him:

(*as herself, to Ian*) What do you mean?

(*as Ian*) Like, around, like… as in, available for hangouts and
general good times.

> *Beat.*

With me.

(*as herself, narrating*) I say yes, and he smiles.

(*as Ian*) Good. Cuz I like it… when you're around.

(*as herself, narrating*) And that's when he kisses me.

Ash and Kate can barely believe it when I start going out with Ian. At first they're kind of awkward around him... like, star-struck. But Ian is so friendly and easy-going, that fades away pretty fast, and pretty soon the four of us are hanging out all the time. Every minute of my time is packed. Creative writing, hanging out with Ian, drama club, sleepovers with Kate and Ash... I fill my time with Good Things. If I can just keep doing that. Fill every minute... maybe this other part of me will go away.

TRANSITION to the field behind the school.

It's late March, and me, Kate, Ash, and Ian are lying on the field behind the school, picking out shapes in the clouds. It's one of Ian's favourite activities.

(*as Ian*) Okay Ash, take it away. What do you see?

(*as Ash*) Hot-air balloon. Too easy. Next.

(*as herself, narrating*) Kate laughs and says:

(*as Kate*) Ash, you can't "next" the clouds, it's the freakin' sky. They just stay there until the wind moves them.

(*as herself, narrating*) Ian moves his hands in front of his face in a square, framing a cloud.

(*as Ian*) Yeah, and besides, Ash... I don't see a hot-air balloon. I see... a Russian circus bear peddling a hilariously small unicycle away from what I think is... yep, it's definitely his leprechaun circus master.

(*as herself, narrating*) Kate laughs, but Ash looks annoyed.

(*as Ash*) Ian Nakamura, you are insane. That is way too detailed for cloud pictures, and anyway it's totally a hot-air balloon. Except it moved, so now it looks more like a hot-air... pickle.

(*as herself, narrating*) Ian brushes some of the hair off my forehead.

(*as Ian*) What do you think, Nina-bean? What do you see?

> *Beat.*

Nina? Hello...

(*as herself, narrating*) I'm not thinking about what the clouds look like, I don't see anything fun up in the sky. I'm thinking about how ever since I got up this morning, my skin didn't feel like it fit. I've been walking around all day trying to get comfortable and feel like myself, but I can't. I don't belong anywhere.

NOT THIS! I thought I was over this! I thought I was back to normal! Stop acting like a freak, Nina, just be with your friends!

(*as Ian*) Nina? You okay?

(*as herself, to Ian*) Fine. Yeah. I'm just over clouds right now. Let's get mochas.

TRANSITION to the therapist's office.

I'm trying to fill my life with Good Things – GOOD THINGS. But nothing works. And it's like... how awful must I be... how ungrateful... to have all this good stuff in my life and still feel like... pounding heart, shallow breath, tight skin. Darkness all the time.

Every day that spring, things get worse. I start visiting my bathroom-stall hiding place as much as possible. Before class, between class, sometimes during class. I just need to be alone. I need things inside me to settle.

TRANSITION *to her bedroom as* NINA *curls into a ball in her chair.*

At the end of the day when I'm finally home, finally alone, in my room... things are... better... I mean... at least I don't have to pretend... I don't have to try to put on some happy, normal face. When I'm all alone, I can just deal with the fact that I'm me. Worthless.

(*as the Creep*) Why are you crying?

(*as herself, narrating*) I stop breathing. I look up at the door and the Creep is standing there. Watching. Intruding.

(*as herself, to the Creep*) What the hell, Creep, you never heard of knocking?

(*as the Creep*) Are you okay?

(*as herself, to the Creep*) Get out of here.

Beat.

Are you deaf?

Beat.

I SAID GET OUT OF HERE, YOU LITTLE LOSER!

He disappears and I slam the door.

NINA tries and fails to calm down; her breath is jagged and panicked.

What's happening to me? My skin... My skin is burning, I feel like I could breathe fire! I want... I want to hurt... someone... I need... I need to – I need to hurt.

The door comes crashing open. It's Little Miss Sunshine.

(*as herself, to Little Miss Sunshine*) YOU'RE SUPPOSED TO KNOCK.

(*as Little Miss Sunshine*) Nina, that is enough. Your brother is in his room crying. Now, I don't know what's going on with you these days, but leave your brother out of it. It is not his responsibility to indulge whatever teenaged melodrama you are currently living through.

(*as herself, narrating*) And she's gone. Door closed. No "chin up," no positive spin. Even Little Miss Sunshine is no match for my darkness. The fire inside me goes out, as quickly as it lit, and I'm just... empty.

NINA writes in her journal.

Where do you go

When the world doesn't fit?

How can you hide from yourself?

There's a picture in my mind

Of a girl I used to know

But I've lost her.

I'm lost.

I'm toxic.

Where do you go when your mind doesn't fit?

When your heart pumps tar?

When your spirit is cracked?

Where do you go when you've lost yourself?

Where do you go?

Where did *I* go?

When did the me that I was disappear?

How can I ever come back?

    NINA closes her journal.

I don't sleep that night. Not one wink. I lie awake and
feel this emptiness fill me from bottom to top. No, not
emptiness. Poison.

In the morning I look like absolute hell, I must, because Little
Miss Sunshine doesn't blink when I say:

(*to Little Miss Sunshine*) I'm sick.

I stay in my room, tucked away. Sick. I don't have a cold or a
fever or a headache... but there's something wrong inside me
and it's eating me alive.

TRANSITION to school.

(*as Kate*) Where. The Hell. Have You. Been?

(*as herself, narrating*) It's my first day back at school since my
fight with the Creep.

(*as Kate*) You missed the best thing last week in drama club!
Mr. Angus said we're going to get a whole half-hour at the all-
school showcase in May! And it's all thanks to you and your
fabulous writing! So get going, Shakespeare! We need some
great stuff from you for the showcase.

(*as herself, narrating*) Good Things. Drama club is a Good Thing.

I become obsessed. I stay up late, I work on the scenes when I should be doing homework. I write and write. I'm always writing.

I'm driving Ian crazy with my drama-club obsession, but I don't care.

(*as Ian*) Maybe we could have an afternoon where we don't talk about drama club? Let's cloud-watch!

(*as herself, to Ian*) Maybe later. I have to focus – I've got a lot of stuff to write. I gotta go home.

TRANSITION to home.

When I get home, Little Miss Sunshine is there, waiting for me, waving a piece of paper in her right hand. The Professor is standing behind her. Both of them look pretty grim.

(*as Little Miss Sunshine*) Do you know what came in the mail today, Nina? An interim report card. You're failing almost every class! How did this happen?

(*as herself, narrating*) She hands me the paper. It's true. My mark in almost every class is sitting somewhere between 35 and 55 percent. I look at the notes from my teachers. It's because I haven't been doing my homework.

The Professor takes the paper, studying it.

(*as the Professor*) How could this happen? You have always been an excellent student! I mean, you're even failing creative writing! It's your favourite class! How is that possible?

(*as herself, narrating*) I look from the Professor to Little Miss Sunshine and back again. I don't have an answer.

(*as Little Miss Sunshine*) You're *failing*, Nina, do you understand that? *Failing*. What do you have to say for yourself?

(*as herself*) I'm sorry. I'm *sorry*.

I'm sorry I'm failing.

I'm sorry I'm bad.

This is what I say in my head. In my head I talk and talk and cry and tell my parents that I don't know what's wrong with me; that I'm scared and I'm lost and I need them now more than I've ever needed anybody in my entire life. But things can happen in your head and never make it to the real world. In the real world, I keep failing. I look back at them both, and I say nothing at all.

TRANSITION to school.

(*as Kate*) I don't get it. You're, like, a total Einstein. How did this even happen?

(*as herself, narrating*) I tell Ash and Kate to meet me early the next day at school so I can tell them about my interim report card. I also have to lay out the Professor and Little Miss Sunshine's "game plan" to get my marks back on track: no drama club until I'm passing all my classes.

(*as Ash*) What the hell! What are we going to do? The all-school showcase is, like, two weeks away and I don't have any lines yet!

(*as herself, narrating*) School ends and I gather my stuff, to head straight home, as per Little Miss Sunshine's orders. Ian stops me.

(*as Ian*) I looked for you all day. Kate told me about what happened with your parents. Are you okay?

(*as herself, to Ian*) I'm... yeah, I'm fine. Here's my writing binder. There's some finished scenes in there. I gotta go.

TRANSITION to home.

At home Little Miss Sunshine sends me straight to my room to get started on all the catch-up work I have to do, and then she heads off to take the Creep to his violin lesson. She's only been gone a few minutes when our doorbell rings.

I look out my bedroom window, and Ian's standing there, pacing back and forth on the porch. That's weird. Why isn't he in drama club? He looks up at my window – his face is pale as a ghost. What's going on?

I race down the stairs to ask him what's wrong, but when I open the door, I can't get a word out before he says:

(*as Ian*) What is this? I found it in your writing binder.

(*as herself, narrating*) He starts to read.

(*as Ian, reading*) Lost in a crowd, feeling alone

You want to speak up, but there's nobody home.

(*as herself, to Ian*) It's nothing. It's private! I didn't mean to give you that. Give it back.

(*as Ian, reading*) What would I lose if I let it all go?

If I disappeared would anyone know?

(*as herself, to Ian*) Go away Ian, I don't want to talk to you!

(*as herself, narrating*) I grab the papers and I slam the door. He's seen what I am.

NINA paces like a cornered animal. She may almost be sick, she may hit herself. She is trying, and failing, to calm herself down.

I go to the bathroom and close the door.

I take out the razor I use to shave my legs. I pull up my sleeve.

I press it into my arm. Nothing happens. I move it back and forth. Nothing. I press harder but the stupid protective plastic casing means it just won't work.

I try to pry the blade out. I can't. I grab the soap dish and I smash the razor. The plastic finally cracks. I get the blade out and think about every dark, bad part of myself as I press it into my arm.

NINA mimes cutting herself once, deliberately.

It hurts. It hurts like it should. It hurts like I deserve! I hate you! I HATE YOU!

The door opens. It's Little Miss Sunshine.

The air goes out of the room. No sound, nothing. It's just me and her... and the blade in my hand.

(*as herself, to Little Miss Sunshine*) Mom...

We sit on my bed and talk and talk. I cry. Mom cries. Talking is scary and hard.

Dad gets home and Mom tells him what happened. He looks at me, this man, this grown-up. His eyes fill up with tears.

TRANSITION back to NINA in her therapist's office, speaking in real time to the therapist.

That was last week. I haven't been back to school since.
My parents walk around the house like things will break
if they move too fast or talk too loud. Every night they tell
me how much they love me. Ian's called me, like, a zillion
times, but I never pick up. He keeps leaving messages and
texting. "Are you okay?" "I'm here for you." "Call me any
time." Yesterday I got a text from Kate. "Is everything okay?
Don't worry about the showcase stuff. Me and Ash just want
to know if you're all right." I haven't written back yet. I don't
know what to say.

Good Things. My life has lots of Good Things... and good
people in it. But every day is still so hard. No matter what
I do, I just keep falling. Further and further... deeper and
deeper into the darkness. I don't want to get stuck here.
I don't want to be... frozen, perfectly still, falling through life.

I tried... I've been trying for so long to figure out how to
handle this on my own, how to fix... whatever this is by
myself. I can't.

I want... I want to find a way to be... myself again... and...
and I need help to do that. Help me. Help me come back to
myself.

Lights fade.

THE END

Still • Falling

(Nick)

PRODUCTION HISTORY

Still • Falling (Nick) was first produced in the spring of 2022 by Green Thumb Theatre in Vancouver, British Columbia, with the following cast and crew:

NICK	Matthew Rhodes
Director	Rachel Aberle
Assistant Director	Leslie Dos Remedios
Company Manager	Melissa McCowell
Set Designer	Ken MacDonald
Discussion Facilitator	Shilpa Narayan
Lighting Designer and Lighting Technical Director	John Webber
Associate Lighting Designer	Michael Hewitt
Audio Engineer	Reza Saeedi
Livestream Technician and Videographer	Peter Carlone

CHARACTERS

NICK, a fifteen-year-old boy. By all outward appearances, he is absolutely "typical." He moves between speaking to the audience, speaking in real time to his therapist, and reliving his story. As he moves through his memories, he moves about his therapist's office space; when he is speaking to his therapist, he returns to his chair. At times he speaks as the other characters in his life, indicated by the character's name in parentheses before the line.

SETTING

The play takes place in Nick's therapist's office. Throughout the play, projections and audio may be used to indicate location changes associated with Nick's memories.

NICK sits in his therapist's office. He takes in his surroundings and then looks across at where his therapist would be sitting. He glances at a clock.

NICK

10:05 a.m. We were supposed to start five minutes ago. It's Tuesday morning and I'm supposed to be in school. There are so many things about being here that feel weird, but that's probably the weirdest. School is super important in my family, like... My mom is the kind of person that schedules dentist appointments at 7 a.m. so that we can fit it in before the first bell.

The door swings open and he walks in. When you hear the word "therapist," there's, like, specific things you think of, right? Y'know... Sigmund Freud... some old dude with suspenders and really bushy eyebrows. This guy is so young, I feel like he got his degree, like, yesterday. He has a beard he spends way too much time on, wire-rimmed glasses, full-sleeve tattoos, and he's carrying a bottle of cold-brew coffee. This is the guy I'm supposed to talk to?

He sits down in the armchair across from me, clicks his pen, and says, "Good morning."

(*to the therapist*) Hi. I mean, good morning. Um... nice office. I mean, I guess it's nice. What do I know?

(*narrating*) I know I sound like an idiot, okay? "Nice office?" What am I even talking about? God, thirty seconds in and I'm already doing this wrong.

(*to the therapist*) What's that? When did I get here? Um... like... ten minutes ago? Remember, I buzzed in? Oh! To Vancouver? Grade ten. I mean, a week and a half before grade ten started.

TRANSITION to the dinner table. NICK indicates his family members as he describes them.

Tuesday night – taco night. Forever and always, from now until the end of time.

The Coach (that's my dad) is at his spot at this end of the table craning his neck to see the baseball game that's still playing in the living room. The Coach is an electrician when it comes to, like, an actual job, but his one true passion is knowing every move his favourite teams should be making.

(*as the Coach*) That's not the play, Martinez!

He's got a sport for every season, and the Sunbeam lets him keep them on during dinner as long as he mutes the TV.

Oh, the Sunbeam sits over here. She's the creator of Taco Tuesdays, Beef Wellington Wednesdays, and Family-Night Fridays – Suzanne Walker, my mother. See, the Coach is always in his own world a bit, keeping track of all his teams' stats, but the Sunbeam is RIGHT HERE, IN YOUR FACE, asking, "How was your day? Would you like a mini quiche?" She's... the life of the party. Even when there is no party.

And right here is my little brother Tyler... the Creep. I'm pretty sure he's an eight-year-old goblin/human hybrid my parents found under a bridge.

(*as the Creep*) I am not a goblin!

(*as himself, like he's caught him*) Spoken like a true goblin!

Then there's me, right here – Nick Walker.

So here we are, halfway through the summer before I start grade ten, tacos assembled, ready to dive in, when suddenly –

(*as the Sunbeam*) Attention, kiddios –

(*as himself, narrating*) I hate when she calls us that.

(*as the Sunbeam*) Your dad and I have some exciting news. Honey – do you want to tell them? Gordon!

(*as himself, narrating*) The Coach's eyes scan from the living room to all of us at the table. It's like we've materialized from nothing and he has no idea who we are.

(*as the Sunbeam*) Honey, I was telling the kids we have news. You want to tell them your exciting announcement?

(*as the Coach*) Uh... right. News. Yes... announcement! We are moving. To Vancouver. In a month.

(*as himself, narrating*) WHAT?!

(*as the Creep*) Yes! British Columbia is home to the *Ariolimax columbianus*!

(*as himself, to the Creep*) What are you talking about?

(*as the Creep*) The Pacific banana slug! Fact! If you lick them, your tongue goes numb!

(*as himself, to the Creep*) What?

(*as the Creep*) Maybe I'll get to lick one!

(*as himself, to the Sunbeam*) Mom! What am I supposed to do? Y'know... friends, school? My life?!

(*as the Coach*) Buck up, Nick. Lotsa kids move. It's not the end of the world.

(*as the Sunbeam*) Nick, I know it might seem like you're going to be giving up a lot. But think about what you'll be gaining. You are going to make so many new friends and try so many new things. We can go skiing! Watch the whales! And the school has a specialized creative-writing program.

(*as himself, in real time to the therapist*) 'Kay, this is a dirty trick. My uncle gave me this book of Leonard Cohen poetry at the beginning of grade nine, and ever since I've been writing a bunch. Just, like... stories and... poems – which is so cringey, I know, but... I don't know... I'm into it. So yeah, a creative writing program sounds cool, but enough to turn my whole world upside down? Not sure about that.

(*as the Sunbeam*) Your life is going to be filled right up with good things. Everything is going to be fine, Nick – better than fine! You are going to *love* Vancouver.

TRANSITION to **NICK** standing in front of his new school, looking up at it.

Vancouver is grey and wet, and the school... the school is huge. Everyone around me knows where they're going and knows each other. I don't know anything. What was the Sunbeam thinking? I don't belong here.

I go to walk into the school. My legs have turned to lead. My heart feels like it's going to burst through my chest. I want to go home, I want to disappear. I want to do anything but walk into this building.

(*giving himself a pep talk*) Think of something good. Come on Nick, buck up. Relax. I can't relax! I can't even breathe!

Suddenly this guy grabs me by the elbow –

(*as Chris, yelling*) What are you doing? Come inside, you're soaking wet!

(*as himself, narrating*) He pulls me through the front door. Once we're inside, he bursts out laughing.

(*as Chris*) What were you doing? You were like a statue
out there.

(*as himself, to Chris*) It's my first day. I don't really know where
I'm going.

(*as Chris*) 'Kay, well, the office is that way. What's your name?

(*as himself, to Chris*) Nick.

(*as Chris*) Cool. See ya.

(*as himself, narrating*) I don't even get his name before he
disappears.

The first two classes go okay. I make it through without
getting lost or – more importantly – turning into a statue
again. At lunch I walk into the cafeteria. It's massive. Then I
start to feel it again – the pounding heart, the shallow breath.

(*as Chris*) Nate! You're alive! How were your first couple
classes?

It's the guy from the beginning of the day. It takes me a
second to understand that he's talking to me.

(*as Chris*) Nate! Nate! Earth to Nate! How's it going?

(*as himself, to Chris*) What? Oh. Hi. Nick. It's Nick.

(*as Chris*) Right, sorry, my bad. Come sit with us! We're only
assholes, like, half the time.

(*as himself, narrating*) He still hasn't told me his name, but
it doesn't take long to figure out. Chris Sidhu. King of the
Cafeteria. Not in a bad way. It just seems like everybody
knows this guy. Knows him and likes him. A few minutes into
lunch, a blond guy with an intense tan and bright-white teeth
shows up and Chris has a couple people shove over to make
some space.

(*as Chris*) Nick, this is Asher. Asher, Nick.

(*as Asher*) Nickelback, what's up?

(*as Chris*) Ash, it's Nick's first day. I found him frozen like a statue outside the school before first bell and it was the most pathetic thing I've ever seen. I'm pretty sure he'll get eaten alive without our guidance and expertise.

(*as Asher*) We got you, Nickelodeon.

TRANSITION to the dinner table.

(*as the Sunbeam*) Attention, Walker family, attention, please! Everyone, raise a glass! A toast to our very first Vancouver Mix-and-Match Monday!

(*as himself, narrating*) Mix-and-Match Monday has always been the Sunbeam's favourite dinner theme night. We're all responsible for making one of the items for dinner. The Creep boiled water – which shouldn't count, OBVIOUSLY, but he gets away with *everything* – I made a salad, the Sunbeam made this fancy stuffed pasta from scratch with pesto and sun-dried tomatoes, and the Coach made his specialty: Oreos®. Double Stuf®.

(*as the Sunbeam*) So! Let's hear it! Worsts and bests! I want a full report!

(*as himself, narrating*) This is another one of the Sunbeam's favourite things. At dinner we all have to share the worst thing that happened to us that day and the best.

(*as the Sunbeam*) All right, Nick, take it away...

(*as himself, narrating*) I start to answer, but when I try to think of a "worst"... all I can think of is being stuck in front of the school... (*beginning to breathe unevenly*) I can't talk about this.

(*as himself, to the Sunbeam*) Um... you better ask Dad... looks like the game's going into extra innings, and I'm pretty sure he's gonna be unreachable.

(*as the Sunbeam*) Gordon! Your presence is requested in reality. Give us a worst and a best!

(*as the Coach*) What? Right, worsts and bests. Worst... jeez. Well, the drywallers here are no better than back home, so I spent most of the afternoon watching them take down sheets they put up over top of a bunch of circuitry I hadn't finished. So... just another day in paradise. Best... well, Ryu is back from his injury, so the Jays have a fighting chance, if they can just... (*looking back at the TV*) Aw, come on!! Out by a *mile*!

(*as himself, narrating*) The Creep pipes up:

(*as the Creep*) I'll go next! Best part: easy. Found a slug after school and I brought it home. Worst part? Now I can't find him.

(*as himself, narrating*) I look over at the Sunbeam. Slug lost somewhere in the house? This is when an ordinary mom would flip out. Instead...

(*as the Sunbeam*) So... family slug hunt after dinner! Great! All right Nick, back to you. Worst and best, what happened today?

(*as himself, to the Sunbeam*) Um... I don't know. I didn't have a "worst."

(*as the Sunbeam*) Excellent! And? Best?

(*as himself, to the Sunbeam*) I guess... I mean, I think I... made some friends?

TRANSITION to school as NICK delivers the
    following lines.

Becoming friends with Chris is, like, a crazy-lucky break.
It's basically like having an answer key to everything about
this school. You name it – he knows it. Where to sit, who to
talk to – and for whatever reason, he feels like sharing it all
with me.

(*as Chris, talking about other people in the hallway as they pass
    by*) That's Charles DeWitt. He's... he's something else. Get
this – last year, we were learning about, like, King Arthur
and Merlin in English, and he ACTUALLY asked if dragons
were extinct. Actually. That's Marissa Choi – she has two
older brothers and her parents go out of town ALL the time,
so we'll definitely go to parties at her house. She's cool. Oh,
and that – okay, put your eyes back in your head. That's Nour
Ahmadi. Super chill, super funny.

(*as himself, narrating*) So as much as I make fun of the
Sunbeam for her motivational speeches and overall
cheerleader attitude, maybe she was right.

In October, me, Chris, and Asher go to the Halloween
dance dressed as the Three Blind Mice. We're all wearing
sunglasses, which Asher refuses to take off.

(*as Ash*) Come on guys, they're integral to the character.
Without them, we're just mice.

(*as himself, narrating*) Only problem is, the lights in the gym
are really dark, so he keeps bumping into everything. At the
end of the night, he locks eyes with Tina Brockton, who
he's been into for, like, forever. He heads over to ask her to
dance, but because he can't see anything he trips over Leon
Goldberg's dragon tail, knocking into the speaker system,

which topples over *directly* on Tina – who breaks her ankle. Needless to say, she doesn't speak to Asher for the rest of the term.

Oh! And creative writing. The class is really cool. We put out a newspaper for the whole school every month, and in December one of my short stories gets picked to be in the paper, which Chris will *not* let go...

(*as Chris*) A writer! It all makes sense now. The brooding stare, the emo aura that hovers over you in every room. Nicholas Walker... Clarke Secondary's own William Shack-a-spear.

(*as Asher*) Who?

(*as Chris*) Shakespeare.

    Beat.

Like... Shakespeare? William Shakespeare.

(*as Ash*) Right. He wrote the book about the big whale.

(*as Chris, to Asher*) Ash, I'm trying to roast Nick here, but your stupidity is making it impossible to focus on my target.

(*as himself, narrating*) By Christmas break I'm feeling really solid. I like this city, I like my friends, and I like my school. Good Things.

TRANSITION to Nick's bedroom.

(*as the Sunbeam, calling from outside Nick's bedroom door*) Nick! Hello! Wakey-wakey, eggs and bakey! Just kidding there's only cereal. Come on! Get up! It's Christmas-Tree Day!

(*as himself, narrating*) It's December twenty-third: Christmas-Tree Day, another important day in Walker Family Tradition.

We all go out two days before Christmas, pick out a tree, bring it home, and decorate it. The only rule is we have to pick out the saddest, rattiest, Charlie-Browniest tree possible, and make it awesome. I know… totally corny… but it's fun.

I'm trying to muster up the energy for Christmas-Tree Day… But this year I'm just… not feeling it.

I didn't sleep too well last night. It's been weird to be home from school. Too much time on my hands.

(*trying to pump himself up*) Whatever. Okay. Let's do this.

I open my drawer and stand there.

Blue shirt, grey shirt. Blue shirt… or grey shirt? Blue shirt, grey shirt. Come on, idiot, this isn't rocket science. Blue shirt… or grey shirt? Jeez, what's wrong with me?

I can't breathe. My skin feels all cold, and… ugh, what the hell? Blue shirt, grey shirt… (*whispering, trying and failing to calm his breath*) Blue shirt grey shirt blue shirt grey shirt… Shit! (*wiping tears from his eyes*) What is going on?

> NICK turns from the closet and goes to write in his journal.

Normal guy

Normal heart

Normal brain

Then it starts

A creeping feeling: sorrow, dread

A tiny voice inside my head

Stay inside, keep out of sight

Something in you isn't right

Venom in you, dark as night

Ugly, shameful, full of spite

Sickened guy

Jagged heart

Crooked mind

Tears you apart

Stupid guy

Broken brain

Ugly heart

Am I insane?

NICK closes his journal, puts it away, and TRANSITIONS
into sitting once again in the therapist's office.

The therapist sits, scratching away on his notepad. He's been
that way since the moment I started talking. Now that I've
stopped for a second, he looks up at me, totally unfazed.
I don't know what I expected... some kind of reaction,
I guess? A raised eyebrow, maybe? But he just looks back at
me silently, waiting for me to continue.

(*to the therapist*) So, I mean... that's totally weird, right?

(*as himself, narrating*) He shrugs his shoulders, like he for real
has no opinion on the matter. I do not get this guy. He's so
freakin'... calm and collected. I might as well be listing off my
top ten favourite foods, or describing a really mediocre sunset
I saw one time.

(*to the therapist*) Pardon? Do *I* think it's weird? Well, like, obviously, or I wouldn't have asked you. Aren't you supposed to be telling me what's weird and what's normal, and, like… what's wrong with me? (*pause as the therapist asks a question*) Well, if I didn't think there was something wrong with me, I wouldn't be here! Isn't that, like, completely obvious? (*pause*) I'm *not* mad, I'm just… whatever. What do you want me to talk about now? Keep going? Fine.

TRANSITION to the family living room.

It's Christmas morning and we're opening gifts.

(*as the Sunbeam*) Is there something you want to say to your brother?

(*as himself, narrating*) I know where I am, but I have no idea what the Sunbeam is talking about.

(*as himself, to the Sunbeam*) Huh?

(*as the Sunbeam*) You've been raised to say "thank you" when someone gives you a gift, Nick.

(*as himself, to the Sunbeam*) What?

(*as himself, narrating*) I look down at my hand. I'm holding a solid-brass banana slug. Life-sized. I look across the living room and the Creep is sitting there, eyes brimming with tears, looking totally defeated.

(*as the Creep*) It's a paperweight. Cuz you like writing. I thought you would like it.

(*as himself, narrating*) I remember opening the thing. I remember thinking, "Say thank you now." But instead I just sat there, staring at the floor. Time stopped. I look up at the Creep.

(*as himself, to the Creep*) I ... I do, man. It's totally awesome. Thank you. For real.

TRANSITION *back to school as* **NICK** *says the*
following lines.

January fifth comes. Finally. Christmas break is supposed to be fun, relaxing, but I just felt like ... sometimes I was on another planet. Other times, it was like ... It was like I was drowning.

It's okay. I just have to stop being such a freak. I know getting back to school will fix this. I'll see my friends, I'll have stuff to do. Both Good Things.

My relief evaporates when Chris announces:

(*as Chris*) You, me, and Asher are all joining drama club.

(*as himself, to Chris*) Wh ... why?

(*as Asher*) Dude, do you know how many girls are in drama club? Tina's got me on the "no" list ever since the speaker incident. I need to diversify my portfolio.

(*as himself, to Asher*) Okay, so ... *you* join drama club.

(*as himself, narrating*) Chris smacks me on the back.

(*as Chris*) Man up, Nick! It's drama club, not a pit of lava. Besides, Asher is nothing without a wingman or two.

(*as himself, to Chris*) I – I'm not an actor! I took creative writing ... It's basically the opposite. We don't stand up in front of people talking, we sit in corners and write all by ourselves.

(*as Chris*) Okay, take a breath, Shakespeare. You don't have to act. You can write stuff for me and Ash to perform. You'll be our secret weapon!

(*as himself, narrating*) And before I know it, we're in the drama room. Because it's the first meeting, we have to go around the room and say why we're here. People say things like:

(*as Chivaun*) Hey, I'm Chivaun... Grade ten. I've just, like... always really respected what acting is about, you know? Like... seeing the world through another person's eyes? I feel like if everyone could do that, the world would be, like, such a better place. Namaste.

(*as himself, narrating*) Everyone's taking it super seriously. Well... almost everyone.

(*as Asher*) I'm Asher. Sagittarius. Are we going to have to kiss for any of the scenes? Like, it's fine if we do. Like, I'm fine with that. Like, if you give me a scene with kissing? That's totally fine. That's just, like... acting, y'know? Hey, Chivaun.

(*as himself, narrating*) And then it's my turn.

(*as himself, to his class*) Hi.

Beat.

I'm Nick.

Beat.

Um, I'm not really into acting.

Beat.

So obviously, drama club was the natural choice.

Beat.

The "Standing Around Awkwardly club" had an epic waitlist.

(*as himself, narrating*) I'm ready for a room of blank stares, but instead people laugh.

(*as himself, to his class*) Okay. So I'll make you guys a deal. I'll write skits for you guys to perform as long as you *never* make me talk in front of a group again. Fair?

(*as himself, narrating*) This girl across the circle from me gives me a huge smile. It's super-hilarious, super-gorgeous Nour Ahmadi. Smiling. At me.

Every meeting we have after that, I make sure that I have some skits ready, and... It never fails. Every meeting, people want to hear my stuff. They all laugh when I hoped they would laugh, and almost always someone comes up to me afterwards to say, "good job." It feels... really good.

TRANSITION to the bathroom, where NICK is hiding, breathing unevenly, trying not to break down sobbing.

I'm in the last stall in the bathroom on the third floor, at the far end of the hall. The one with the chipped paint around the lock and the graffiti that says "Marcus was here" next to "Grad 2017." I'm here because nobody ever comes into this bathroom. I'm here because I'm... I'm losing my mind.

What is wrong with me? Everything's been great since school started back up, since I can see my friends again, since things have been going well in drama club, but today, it's just like Christmas break. Today...

I didn't want to come to school today. The moment my eyes opened today, I knew that I needed to stay home. I TOLD the Sunbeam that I wasn't feeling well, but she took my temperature and when it was fine the Coach gave his standard "buck up," and that was that.

NICK takes a moment to compose himself.

I come out of the stall and I look in the mirror. That's when I see it. What everyone else must see. Me. Total loser panic-stricken freak. Weak. And stupid. Weak and stupid. Weak... stupid!

NICK slaps himself in the face. It shocks him.

(*slapping*) Weak! (*slapping*) Stupid!

NICK breathes heavily, working to regain his composure.

TRANSITION to the therapist's office. NICK responds to questions from the therapist.

I wouldn't call it "hiding out." It's a bathroom... It's a public place. I just go there to... take a break.

Beat.

I don't know! A break from everything, I guess.

Beat.

No, that's the point, I don't know why I needed a break... I never know why. This is so stupid. It didn't happen a lot, okay? At first it was just now and then.

TRANSITION back to school. NICK is at his locker.

After drama club one day, I feel a tap on my shoulder. Holy crap! It's Nour Ahmadi.

(*as Nour*) Nick, what's up? I liked what you wrote today. You're funny.

(*as himself, to Nour*) Thanks.

(*as Nour*) So you wanna write something brilliant for me? We could work on it together.

(*as himself, narrating*) I don't know what to say. Or I mean I do – YES! YES, LET'S TOTALLY DO THAT! But it's like I'm frozen to the spot, the words just won't come. Nour starts to turn to go.

(*as Nour*) Okay, never mind, no sweat...

(*as himself, to Nour, shouting*) Wait! (*at a normal level, trying to regain his cool*) Um, I mean... hold up.

(*as Nour*) I was starting to think you might be a mime.

(*as himself, to Nour*) Yes! Yes. I mean, no! I'm not a mime. But um, yes. We should totally work on scenes together.

(*as Nour*) Cool. Want to meet up today after school? I'll pick you up. Seriously, I'm very strong. Like... freakishly. It's a problem. (*laughing*) Jokes. No, I'll uh... I'll come to your locker and then we can both walk in the same direction at the same time... Sound good?

(*as himself, narrating*) Nour is... really nice. That first afternoon we go to this coffee shop near school and talk about scenes I could write for her. I'm taking notes on everything we talk about, but after a while, Nour reaches over and closes my binder.

(*as Nour*) Okay, I have a confession. I had a selfish reason for wanting to hang out with you today. I... You're interesting. Like... who are you? I feel like you have a secret identity.

(*as himself, narrating*) When she says this, she looks me right in the eye, like she's looking for something. Looking for my secrets. And just like that, I'm not in the coffee shop anymore. I'm in the bathroom on the third floor again, hiding out, hitting myself in the face. Freak! I am such a freak, and she knows. She can see everything I've been trying to hide. I know it.

(*as Nour*) So, are you going to be around this weekend?

(*as himself, narrating*) I ask her:

(*as himself, to Nour*) What do you mean?

(*as Nour*) Like, around, like... as in, available for hangouts and general good times.

    Beat.

With me.

(*as himself, narrating*) I say yes, and she smiles.

(*as Nour*) Good. Cuz I like it... when you're around.

(*as himself, narrating*) And that's when she kisses me.

Asher and Chris can barely believe it when I start going out with Nour.

(*as Asher*) Let me get this straight. *I'm* the one that said we should join drama club, and you're the one who winds up with a girlfriend? Criminal.

(*as himself, narrating*) Every minute of my time is packed. Creative writing, hanging out with Nour, drama club, weekends with Chris and Asher... I fill my time with Good Things. If I can just keep doing that. Fill every minute... maybe this other part of me will go away.

TRANSITION to the field behind the school.

It's late March, and me, Chris, Asher, and Nour are lying on the field behind the school, picking out shapes in the clouds. It's one of Nour's favourite activities.

(*as Nour*) Okay Asher, take it away. What do you see?

(*as Asher*) Hot-air balloon. Too easy. Next.

(*as himself, narrating*) Chris laughs and says:

(*as Chris*) Ash, you can't "next" the clouds, it's the freakin' sky. They just stay there until the wind moves them.

(*as himself, narrating*) Nour moves her hands in front of her face in a square, framing a cloud.

(*as Nour*) Yeah and besides, Ash… I don't see a hot-air balloon. I see… a Russian circus bear, peddling a hilariously small unicycle away from what I think is… yep, it's definitely his leprechaun circus master.

(*as himself, narrating*) Chris laughs, but Asher looks annoyed.

(*as Asher*) Nour Ahmadi. Please. That is way too detailed for cloud pictures, and anyway it's obviously a hot-air balloon. Except it moved, so now it looks more like a hot-air… pickle.

(*as himself, narrating*) Nour turns to me.

(*as Nour*) What about you, Nick? What do you see?

    Beat.

    Nick? Hello…

(*as himself, narrating*) I'm not thinking about what the clouds look like, I don't see anything fun up in the sky. I'm thinking about how ever since I got up this morning, my skin didn't feel like it fit. I've been walking around all day trying to get comfortable and feel like myself, but I can't. I don't belong anywhere.

NOT THIS! I thought I was over this! I thought I was back to normal! Stop acting like a freak, Nick, just be with your friends!

(*as Nour*) Nick? You okay?

(*as himself, to Nour*) Fine. Yeah. I'm just over clouds right now. Let's get out of here.

TRANSITION to the therapist's office.

I'm trying to fill my life with Good Things – GOOD THINGS. But nothing works. And it's like... How awful must I be... how pathetic... to have all this good stuff in my life and still feel this... pounding heart, shallow breath, tight skin. So weak.

Every day that spring, things get worse. I start visiting my bathroom-stall hiding place as much as possible. Before class, between class, sometimes during class. I just need to be alone. I need things inside me to settle.

TRANSITION to his bedroom as NICK curls into a ball in his chair.

At the end of the day when I'm finally home, finally alone, in my room... things are... better... I mean... at least I don't have to pretend... I don't have to try to put on some happy, normal face. When I'm all alone, I can just deal with the fact that I'm me. Worthless.

(*as the Creep*) Why are you crying?

(*as himself, narrating*) I stop breathing. I look up at the door and the Creep is standing there. Watching. Intruding.

(*as himself, to the Creep*) What the hell, Creep, you never heard of knocking?

(*as the Creep*) Are you okay?

(*as himself, to the Creep*) Get out of here.

> *Beat.*

Are you deaf?

> *Beat.*

I SAID GET OUT OF HERE, YOU LITTLE LOSER!

(*as himself, narrating*) He disappears and I slam the door.

> **NICK** *tries and fails to calm down; his breath is jagged and panicked.*

What's happening to me? My skin... My skin is burning, I feel like I could breathe fire! I want... I want to hurt... I need... I need to – I need to hurt.

The door comes crashing open. It's the Sunbeam.

(*as himself, to the Sunbeam*) YOU'RE SUPPOSED TO KNOCK.

(*as the Sunbeam*) Nick, that is enough. Your brother is in his room crying. Now, I don't know what's going on with you these days, but leave your brother out of it. It is not his responsibility to indulge whatever teenaged melodrama you are currently living through.

(*as himself, narrating*) And she's gone. Door closed. No "chin up," no positive spin. Even the Sunbeam is no match for my gloom. The fire inside me goes out, as quickly as it lit, and I'm just... empty.

    NICK writes in his journal.

Where do you go

When the world doesn't fit?

How can you hide from yourself?

There's a picture in my mind

Of a guy I used to know

But I've lost him

I'm lost

I'm toxic.

Where do you go when your mind doesn't fit

When your heart pumps tar

When your spirit is cracked?

Where do you go when you've lost yourself?

Where do you go?

Where did *I* go?

When did the me that I was disappear?

How can I ever come back?

    He closes his journal.

I don't sleep that night. Not one wink. I lie awake and feel this emptiness fill me from bottom to top. No, not emptiness. Poison.

In the morning I look like absolute hell, I must, because the Sunbeam doesn't blink when I say:

(*to the Sunbeam*) I'm sick.

I stay in my room, tucked away. Sick. I don't have a cold or a fever or a headache... but there's something wrong inside me, and it's eating me alive.

TRANSITION to school.

(*as Chris*) Where the hell have you been?

(*as himself, narrating*) It's my first day back at school since my fight with the Creep.

(*as Chris*) 'Kay, there's a lot to catch you up on. First of all, Tina Brockton actually acknowledged Asher's existence yesterday for the first time since Speakergate.

(*as Asher*) Hope lives, St. Nicholas.

(*as Chris*) Also, Mr. Angus said that drama club is getting a whole half-hour at the all-school showcase in May. So you gotta get to work on some stuff so Ash and I don't look like complete idiots. Well... so I don't. There's pretty much no hope for Ash.

(*as himself, narrating*) Good Things. Drama club is a Good Thing.

I become obsessed. I stay up late, I work on the scenes when I should be doing homework. I write and write. I'm always writing.

I'm driving Nour crazy with my drama-club obsession, but I don't care.

(*as Nour*) Maybe we could have an afternoon where we don't talk about drama club? Let's cloud watch!

(*as himself, to Nour*) Maybe later. Sorry. I have to focus. But I'll see you tomorrow?

TRANSITION to home.

When I get home, the Sunbeam is there, waiting for me, waving a piece of paper in her right hand. The Coach is standing behind her. Both of them look pretty grim.

(*as the Sunbeam*) Do you know what came in the mail today, Nick? An interim report card. You're failing almost every class! How did this happen?

(*as himself, narrating*) She hands me the paper. It's true. My mark in almost every class is sitting somewhere between 35 and 55 percent. I look at the notes from my teachers. It's because I haven't been doing my homework.

The Coach takes the paper, studying it.

(*as the Coach*) How could this happen? You've always been a great student! I mean, you're even failing creative writing! It's your favourite class! What's the deal, kid?

(*as himself, narrating*) I look from the Coach to the Sunbeam, and back again. I don't have an answer.

(*as the Sunbeam*) You're *failing*, Nick, do you understand that? What do you have to say for yourself?

(*as himself, to the Sunbeam*) I'm sorry. I'm *sorry*.

I'm sorry I'm failing.

I'm sorry I'm bad.

I'm sorry I'm weak.

This is what I say in my head. In my head I talk and talk and tell my parents that I don't know what's wrong with me; that I'm scared and I'm lost and I need them now more than I've ever needed anybody in my entire life. But things can happen in your head and never make it to the real world. In the real world, I keep failing. I look back at them both, and I say nothing at all.

TRANSITION to school.

(*as Chris*) I don't get it. You're a total Einstein. How did this even happen?

(*as himself, narrating*) I tell Asher and Chris to meet me early the next day at school so I can tell them about my interim report card. I also have to lay out the Coach and the Sunbeam's "game plan" to get my marks back on track: no drama club until I'm passing all my classes.

(*as Asher*) What the hell! What are we going to do? The all-school showcase is, like, two weeks away and I don't have any lines yet!

(*as himself, narrating*) School ends and I gather my stuff to head straight home, as per the Sunbeam's orders. Nour stops me.

(*as Nour*) I looked for you all day. Chris told me about what happened with your parents. Are you okay?

(*as himself, to Nour*) I'm... yeah, I'm fine. Here's my writing binder. There's some finished scenes in there. I gotta go.

TRANSITION to home.

At home the Sunbeam sends me straight to my room to get started on all the catch-up work I have to do, and then she heads off to take the Creep to his violin lesson. They've only been gone a few minutes when our doorbell rings.

I look out my bedroom window, and Nour's standing there, pacing back and forth on the porch. That's weird. Why isn't she in drama club? She looks up at my window – all the blood has drained from her face. What's going on?

I race down the stairs to ask her what's wrong, but when I open the door I can't get a word out before she says:

(*as Nour*) What is this? I found it in your writing binder.

(*as himself, narrating*) She starts to read.

(*as Nour, reading*) Lost in a crowd, feeling alone

You want to speak up, but there's nobody home

(*as himself, to Nour*) It's nothing. It's private! I didn't mean to give you that. Give it back.

(*as Nour, reading*) What would I lose if I let it all go?

If I disappeared would anyone know?

(*as himself, to Nour*) Nour, just… just go away, okay? I don't want to talk to you!

(*as himself, narrating*) I grab the papers and I slam the door. She's seen what I am.

> NICK *paces like a cornered animal. He may almost be sick, he may hit himself, he may whisper "buck up, buck up." He is trying, and failing, to calm himself down.*

I go to the bathroom and close the door.

I reach for a razor. I pull up my sleeve.

I press it into my arm. Nothing happens. I move it back and forth. Nothing. I press harder but the stupid protective plastic casing means it just won't work.

I try to pry the blade out. I can't. I grab the soap dish and I smash the razor. The plastic finally cracks. I get the blade out and think about every stupid, weak part of myself as I press it into my arm.

NICK mimes cutting himself once, deliberately.

It hurts. It hurts like it should. It hurts like I deserve! I hate you! I HATE YOU!

The door opens. It's the Sunbeam.

All the air goes out of the room. No sound, nothing. It's just me and her... and the blade in my hand.

(*as himself, to the Sunbeam*) Mom...

We sit on my bed and talk, and talk. I cry. Mom cries. Talking is hard and... terrifying.

Dad gets home and Mom tells him what happened. He looks at me, this man... this strong man. His eyes fill up with tears.

TRANSITION back to NICK in his therapist's office, speaking in real time to the therapist.

That was last week. I haven't been back to school since. My parents walk around the house like things will break if they move too fast or talk too loud. Every night they tell me how much they love me. Nour's called me, like, a zillion times, but I never pick up. She keeps leaving messages and texting. "Are you okay?" "I'm here for you." "Call me any time." Yesterday I got a text from Chris. "Buddy, you okay? You need anything, say the word. We love you." I haven't written back yet. I don't know what to say.

Good Things. My life has lots of Good Things... and good people in it. But every day is still so hard. No matter what I do, I just keep falling. Further and further... deeper and deeper. I don't want to get stuck here. I don't want to be... frozen, perfectly still, falling through life.

I tried... I've been trying for so long to figure out how to handle this on my own, how to fix... whatever this is by myself. I can't.

I want... I want to find a way to be... myself again... and... and I need help to do that. Help me. Help me come back to myself.

Lights fade.

THE END

The Code

PRODUCTION HISTORY

The Code was first produced in the spring of 2018 by Green Thumb Theatre in Vancouver, British Columbia, with the following cast and crew:

MOIRA	Elizabeth Barrett
SIMON	Nathan Kay
CONNOR	Mason Temple
Director	Patrick McDonald
Assistant Director	Bronwyn Carradine
Set Designer	Ruth Bruhn
Costume/Sound Designer	Elizabeth Wellwood
Stage Manager	Tessa Gunn

The Code was developed with support from the 2017 Banff Playwrights Lab at the Banff Centre for Arts and Creativity.

CHARACTERS

MOIRA, a grade-eleven student, a high achiever with a strong sense of justice and an oddball sense of humour.

SIMON, a grade-eleven student, a romantic. Hopelessly smitten with Moira.

CONNOR, a grade-eleven student, slacker, and wannabe ladies' man.

SETTING

The play takes place at the Pit, Moira, Simon, and Connor's dingy but comfortable hangout spot outside their high school. May be made up of benches, curbs, picnic tables, etc. Should contain a garbage can.

NOTE ON OVERLAPPING DIALOGUE

"//" is used in this text to indicate a point at which one character's dialogue overlaps another's.

SCENE 1

MOIRA and CONNOR enter, chatting.

MOIRA
'Kay – do, dump, or marry –

CONNOR
Hit me.

MOIRA
Sardines, liver and onions –

CONNOR
Oh, come on!

MOIRA
Or...

CONNOR
No!

MOIRA
Ketchup chips.

CONNOR
You're the worst at this game!

MOIRA
Do, dump, or marry?

CONNOR
Moira, you can't play with foods.

MOIRA
Answer!

CONNOR
And you're supposed to give at least one that's tolerable.

MOIRA
Ketchup chips are tolerable.

CONNOR
Ketchup chips are Satan's snack food.

MOIRA
I'm waiting.

CONNOR
Ugh, fine. Do: liver and onions.

MOIRA
What!

CONNOR
Dump: ketchup chips. Gross.

MOIRA
Rude.

CONNOR
Marry: sardines, I guess.

MOIRA
That's nuts. Ketchup chips are so NOT the worst of those options.

CONNOR
Whatever. You know my feelings on the subject. You want to play the game properly? Count me in. You want to play your weirdo version with food – save it for Simon.

MOIRA
(*laughing*) Where is he, anyway?

CONNOR
I dunno, text him.

MOIRA
Where's your phone?

CONNOR
Castellano jacked it when I wouldn't stop live-streaming his sex-ed class.

MOIRA
Very mature, Connor.

CONNOR
It had to be done! The man put a condom over his hand and pulled it all the way down to his elbow. Brutal.

MOIRA
(*texting*) So how long are you cut off from civilization?

CONNOR
He said I can pick it up after school.

MOIRA
Oh, so you actually have to go to bio today.

CONNOR
Kind of a bad look if I skip and Ms. Fung sees me.

MOIRA
I don't know… I mean at this point, she may not even know what you look like anymore.

CONNOR
What's the point in going? Class participation is only worth 5 percent. And thanks to you, I've got the best notes in grade eleven.

MOIRA
Y'know, I should cut you off.

CONNOR
Don't even joke about that.

MOIRA
'Kay, do, dump, or marry –

CONNOR
No, no more gross food!

MOIRA
A ferret...

CONNOR
What?

MOIRA
A snake... or an anteater.

CONNOR
I don't even know what an anteater looks like.

MOIRA
Oh, hold on.

MOIRA quickly googles on her phone.

My stepdad just watched a *Planet Earth* on them, and they are his new obsession. Here.

MOIRA shows CONNOR her phone.

CONNOR
Woah. WOAH! Look at his tongue! That's... I feel weird.

MOIRA
Do, dump, or marry?

CONNOR
You are such a freak.

MOIRA
You want my bio notes or not?

CONNOR
Marry the snake.

MOIRA
What?!

CONNOR
Snakes are badass.

MOIRA
Gross.

CONNOR
Do the ferret... Dump that freak show.

MOIRA
Aw, I think they're cute! I would totally marry the anteater.

CONNOR
You are the weirdest person I know. Hand over your notes.

MOIRA
Okay, but don't crease them this time!

> *MOIRA rummages through her bag to retrieve her biology notes as SIMON enters. He films MOIRA and CONNOR on his phone as he speaks to them.*

SIMON
Hola, amigos.

MOIRA
Hola. Hey – boo! No filming!

SIMON
No, this is important, I have an interview to conduct.

MOIRA

Simon, nobody wants to watch a documentary about high school. Term papers and cologne? Boring.

SIMON

Quiet on set. Camera one rolling. Action. Connor McKinnon – how did it go this morning? With the volleyball team?

CONNOR

No way man, I'm not going on the record about this.

MOIRA

Volleyball team?

SIMON

Come on, Connor – I think you make a very compelling subject!

CONNOR

Duh. But I gotta maintain an air of mystery, man.

MOIRA

What about the volleyball team?

CONNOR

I'll explain once he calls "cut."

MOIRA

Simon!

SIMON

Fine. Cut!

> *SIMON turns off the camera on his phone.*

Okay – this morning. Go.

CONNOR

It was a waste of time.

SIMON
How so?

CONNOR
They're out of town all week – tournament.

SIMON
(*laughing*) Classic.

MOIRA
Hello! Still have no idea what anyone's talking about. Explain.

SIMON
So, Casanova here had this brilliant plan –

CONNOR
All right –

SIMON
To stake out the hall around the girls' locker room so he could charm the volleyball team when they got out of morning practice.

MOIRA
Oh, Connor.

CONNOR
Leon tipped me off! *That's* how he got with Jessica. *Nobody* gets with Jessica! Two, three strategic mornings walking her to class – boom! Him and Jessica, up close and personal at Jeff Lee's house party.

SIMON
Classy.

MOIRA
Wait – don't you have a spare first period?

SIMON
Hence the wasted morning.

MOIRA
You got up early to stake out the volleyball team and they aren't even here?

CONNOR
Well, I didn't know that!

MOIRA
And that's what you wore?!

CONNOR
Hey. You may judge my methods, but the outfit don't quit.

MOIRA
Yeah, I wouldn't want that on film.

SIMON
You don't want anything on film.

MOIRA
I'm not made for the big screen.

SIMON
I think you are.

MOIRA
Anyway, Connor, tip for next time – if you're gonna be a low-grade stalker, you at least want to get the details right.

CONNOR
All right, so it wasn't a perfect plan –

MOIRA
Who do you even like on the team?

CONNOR
Who's not to like?

SIMON
Boom.

MOIRA
You don't even have a specific person in mind?

CONNOR
I'm keeping my options open!

SIMON
Oh yeah – they're open all right. Wiiiiide open. (*calling out, pointing at CONNOR*) Hey, any takers? Connor McKinnon's wide open for offers of extracurricular attention –

CONNOR
Shut up!

SIMON
So, uh, anyone interested… Anyone? Hello? (*echoing himself*) Hello, hello, hello…

MOIRA
Poor Connor – no one appreciates your unique… uniqueness.

CONNOR
What about you, Simon. How's it going with your potential bae?

MOIRA
Whaaaaaaat?

SIMON
I don't have a potential bae.

CONNOR
I thought you mentioned someone…

SIMON
Nope.

MOIRA

Don't be bashful! I can't set you up with anyone if I don't know who you like.

SIMON

I don't like anyone.

MOIRA

All right. That's fine. You don't want to talk about it, we can drop it.

SIMON

Thank you.

MOIRA

It's Laura Siemens, isn't it?

SIMON

Wha– no.

MOIRA

Okay, okay, okay – I got this... Carly!

SIMON

No!

CONNOR

Ice cold, Moi. Hint: It isn't anybody he's tutored –

SIMON

Ice cold because it isn't anybody! Period! Now can we drop Connor's weird fantasy delusion and get back to the real world?

SIMON rummages in his bag for something and produces a see-through container with a cupcake inside.

MOIRA

Red Velvet?! What is this magic??

SIMON

Last one at the band bake sale. It's kinda squished.

SIMON offers MOIRA the cupcake. She takes it enthusiastically.

MOIRA

I love you, I love you, I love you! Connor, you want a bite?

CONNOR

Cream-cheese icing – ew.

MOIRA

(*eating*) Do, dump, or marry –

CONNOR

Enough!

MOIRA

(*laughing*) Cream-cheese icing, ketchup chips...

CONNOR

You're a bad person.

MOIRA

And an anteater.

CONNOR

Those aren't even in the same category! 'Kay, Simon – do, dump, or marry –

SIMON

Hit me.

CONNOR

Marissa Choi –

MOIRA
No, no, no – no people.

CONNOR
Why not?

MOIRA
Cuz it's weird, we know them.

CONNOR
So?

MOIRA
So I don't want to think about Simon "doing" Marissa.

SIMON
Jealous?

MOIRA
Ew, no.

CONNOR
What's the big deal, then?

MOIRA
Just, don't talk about girls that way, it's gross.

CONNOR
The game is *supposed* to be played with people, Moi.

MOIRA
Boring. The way I play it is much more philosophical.

CONNOR
Oh yeah, you're very deep.

MOIRA
I know. It must be very intimidating.

> *MOIRA's phone buzzes. She reads a text.*

Crap – I gotta go.

SIMON

What's up?

MOIRA

Janice just texted me "Dance Committee Crisis." So – who knows? It's probably nothing. Janice just keeps trying to find "issues" to take on, cuz she's still jealous that *I* got elected Social Affairs Rep, and she's just our grade rep.

CONNOR

'Kay – I guess I'll see you in bio.

SIMON

You're actually going?

CONNOR

Castellano has my phone.

SIMON

Sex-ed video?

CONNOR

Yeah, boi.

SIMON

Nice.

MOIRA

(*gesturing to her notes*) Cram those notes, bro.

CONNOR

Yes, Mom.

SIMON

After school: *Murder, She Wrote*?

MOIRA

Obviously!

CONNOR
I can't believe you guys watch that show.

MOIRA
It's amazing. The woman has witnessed, like, two hundred plus murders – no sign of PTSD.

CONNOR
Again I say it – you are the weirdest person I know.

MOIRA
If you're gonna do something, do it 100 percent. Peace, hermanos.

CONNOR
Peace.

SIMON
Bye.

> *MOIRA exits. SIMON watches her go.*

CONNOR
Red Velvet cupcake. Nice. Question – have you tried just following her around and whispering, "I secretly love you"?

SIMON
Shut up.

CONNOR
I'm just saying – if the not-so-subtle gestures aren't doing the trick, maybe grow a pair and do something?

SIMON
I am doing something, okay? I'm laying a foundation.

CONNOR
You're getting friend zoned.

SIMON
No, I'm not.

SIMON's phone buzzes. He looks at it.

Ha! See? Cupcake emoji! What does that say to you?! That's flirting.

CONNOR
I mean… maybe.

SIMON's phone buzzes again.

SIMON
Okay, now look at that. Cupcake, heart, cupcake, heart. Hearts, dude!

CONNOR
Yellow hearts. Until you get some action, or at least go on a real date –

SIMON
We go on dates.

CONNOR
Watching a crappy show from the eighties about an old woman who solves murders doesn't count.

SIMON
We do other stuff.

CONNOR
None of it counts if *she* doesn't know they're dates. You're living in the friend zone.

SIMON
Whatever.

CONNOR

Why d'you want to tie yourself down, anyway? We're sixteen! We should be, like... out there, sowing wild oats like a couple of stags!

SIMON

Stags farm oats?

CONNOR

It's an expression.

SIMON

Yeah, I'm not sure it is.

CONNOR

You're not gonna see me getting hung up on one girl. Too many fish in the sea to retire the SS *Connor* to a single port.

SIMON

You're a boat now? I thought you were an oat-farming stag.

CONNOR

I'm a complex man, Simon. All things to all people.

SIMON

Has anyone ever told you you're a colossal idiot?

CONNOR

Daily.

The bell goes. SIMON and CONNOR gather up their stuff.

Moira's the weirdo, I'm the idiot. And you're the delusional one.

SIMON

I'm not delusional.

CONNOR

I'm just saying – ask her on a real date, and we'll talk.

SIMON and CONNOR exit.

SCENE 2

After school. MOIRA enters, talking heatedly on her phone.

MOIRA

Like I didn't think of that... Believe me, I tried. I was, like, "We're a very responsible student body, I think those problems can be handled on a case-by-case basis." She didn't go for it.

SIMON enters, filming. He films MOIRA for a moment, but when he realizes this is a heated situation, he puts the camera away.

MOIRA

That's totally unfair, Janice! I wasn't even a part of the conversations. I'm as surprised as everyone else. Well, if you tell people that, you're straight up lying. Yes, you – hello?

MOIRA sees the call has been ended.

(*to SIMON*) Hey, I don't think I can do *Murder, She Wrote* this afternoon. I'm dealing with a dance committee meltdown.

SIMON

What's going on?

MOIRA

Did you see the dress-code posters?

SIMON

The ones with all the dresses with the Xs over them?

MOIRA

Bingo. They went up during lunch while I was out here with you guys. That's what Janice was texting about.

SIMON

I didn't really look, cuz it was all dresses.

MOIRA

Well, it's Principal Weaver's newest initiative.

SIMON

Don't we already have a dress code?

MOIRA

For school. This one's specifically for dances. Remember how Leon and Jeff and those guys got kind of out of hand at the last dance? Like, crowding certain girls and stuff?

SIMON

Yeah?

MOIRA

Well, Ms. Weaver thinks this will help. She said if girls are dressed more modestly, guys won't be tempted to behave badly. And now a bunch of girls think that because I'm in charge of planning dances, I helped come up with it.

SIMON

That's crazy.

MOIRA

That's what I said! But Janice is totally spreading the story, because she wants me to look bad.

SIMON

Cuz she's mad that you're minister of social studies!

MOIRA

Social affairs rep, yes.

SIMON

Talk about petty. She's an evil genius.

MOIRA

I know!

MOIRA's phone buzzes.

Great. Now girls are posting about it and tagging me! (*reading*) "Trust someone as frigid as @MagicMoi with our dances, don't be surprised when they make us dress like nuns." It's all over my mentions. "Hey @MagicMoi – I wore a floor-length dress to winter formal, still got groped by @Leon500 – how come no rules for guys in your stupid code?"

SIMON

Hey – it's gonna be okay. We just gotta figure out a way to make people understand you didn't have anything to do with creating the rules.

MOIRA

Like how?

SIMON

We'll tell people. Don't stress – people know you throw a good dance, dress code or no. Winter formal was awesome.

MOIRA

Whatever.

SIMON

Moira, c'mon. It's going to be a killer dance. Okay?

Beat.

Okay?? Moi, don't do this to yourself. You deserve to have an amazing night. Um – let's get a limo!

MOIRA
A limo?

SIMON
Why not? It'll be great – my treat. I still have a chunk of change left over from working at camp last summer.

MOIRA
Simon, I'm not gonna let you pay for a limo.

SIMON
You don't have a choice. I insist.

MOIRA
Um... Okay! Okay, it's a date.

SIMON
Great!

MOIRA
But let me buy dinner – we can get the limo to pick us up at the Golden Dragon.

SIMON
Deal.

MOIRA
Thanks, Simon.

SIMON
For what?

MOIRA
You're just good at being a person.

SIMON
Sixteen years of practice.

MOIRA's phone buzzes with another notification.

SIMON
Come on. Put your phone away, and let's go watch an old lady solve a crime.

MOIRA
Okay.

SIMON and MOIRA exit.

SCENE 3

CONNOR enters and takes a seat, doing something on his cellphone. SIMON enters.

SIMON
Bro.

CONNOR
Brosef.

SIMON
Got your phone back, I see.

CONNOR
Yep. Where's Moi, what am I doing here forty-five minutes before first bell?

SIMON
I'm not totally sure, something to do with the dress code.

CONNOR
Oh yeah! Did you see Janice's hashtag?

SIMON
#BreakHerCode, I know. Moi came over yesterday and we tried to watch *Murder, She Wrote*, but her phone kept blowing up with notifications. People are pissed.

CONNOR

Can't blame 'em. Dance is gonna suck.

SIMON

Hey, I don't think it's gonna suck. I, uh, actually think it might be a pretty great night.

CONNOR

What's going on with you? I'm barely awake, and you came in looking like the cat that ate the parrot.

SIMON

Canary.

CONNOR

You know what I mean –

SIMON

Y'know, it's not a big thing. Just… I asked Moira if she wanted to go to the dance together and she totally said yes.

CONNOR

Dude!

SIMON

I know!

CONNOR

I can't believe it! You grew testicles! I mean, personally, I reached puberty years ago, but hey – these things happen at different times for all of us.

SIMON

All right, all right.

CONNOR

No dude – actually – that's very cool.

SIMON

Yeah, it's not bad.

CONNOR

So you must have some idea why Moira wants to meet.
I mean, now that's she's your girlfriend –

SIMON

She's not. Don't make a big thing of this, okay?

CONNOR

Hey – I'm cool as a frozen cucumber, bro. I just want to know
why I'm cutting down on my beauty sleep.

SIMON

It's gonna have something to do with convincing people
she didn't come up with the dress code. That was her big
obsession yesterday afternoon. And y'know, when Moira gets
obsessed with something –

CONNOR

Time stops until the issue is resolved.

SIMON

Exactly. We didn't come up with anything while she was at
my place, but then after dinner I got a text from her saying "I
got it" with, like, twelve snail emojis.

CONNOR

Yeah – what does that mean when she texts the snail emoji?
I asked her if she wanted to get pizza the other day and she
just texted back a snail.

SIMON

It's just her general like – positive icon. Like a happy face.

CONNOR

But a snail.

SIMON
Yeah.

CONNOR
God, she's weird.

SIMON
(*laughing*) Yeah.

MOIRA enters.

MOIRA
Hey guys! Sorry I'm late. Our printer ran out of ink, like, three weeks ago, so I had to stop at Staples, but the prices there are bonkers, so then I went across the street to this weird, very sketchy, all black-and-white printer, and at first they printed everything the wrong size and wanted to charge me for it, but then I cried and they did it again properly for free. So anyway, sorry.

CONNOR
Woah, okay, you're at, like, maximum Moira right now, and it's way too early for that.

Tell me why I'm out of bed.

MOIRA proudly presents each of them with a flyer.

CONNOR
(*reading*) "Our bodies, our clothes, stand up, #BreakOurCode."

SIMON
What is this?

CONNOR
Woah! You want people to do a walkout?

SIMON
Where is this coming from?

MOIRA

I was thinking about what you said, about how I need to find
a way to convince people that I didn't make the dress code
up, and meanwhile my phone was blowing up with people
yelling at me about it, and then Janice's hashtag took off and I
was, like, that's it! Break our code! A protest!

CONNOR

Very anti-establishment, Moi. Didn't know you had it in you.

MOIRA

So I figure if we split up, we can get these stuffed into most
lockers before first bell.

CONNOR

Woah, woah, woah, Che. Look, I support you and
everything, damn the man, whatever, but I'm tired. And I
was gonna skip English anyway, so if it's all the same to you,
I'm going back home.

MOIRA

Connor, have you even looked at the dress code?

CONNOR

I skimmed it. I mean, it doesn't really affect me.

MOIRA

Take another look. I put it on the back of the flyer.

CONNOR

(*reading the dress code*) No spaghetti straps, no tube tops –
I love tube tops – skirts... skirts must be at least four inches
longer than the length of a fully outstretched arm... what
does that even mean?

> *CONNOR starts measuring what a skirt would look
> like on his body.*

SIMON

Won't you get in trouble for this?

MOIRA

I just did an entire unit on civil disobedience in humanities. Why do they teach us this stuff if they don't want us to learn from it?

SIMON

I'm not sure this is what they had in mind.

CONNOR

(*still reading the dress code*) No short shorts?! Too far, Weaver!

MOIRA

Still think the dress code has nothing to do with you?

CONNOR

Short shorts have everything to do with me.

MOIRA

(*dividing up the flyers*) Okay, so you take a third, and you take a third...

SIMON

So wait a minute, you want people to just go stand around in a field? What's that gonna do?

MOIRA

I brought some notes on things to say. And a megaphone.

CONNOR

Man, even when you break the rules, you're a total nerd.

SIMON

What are you gonna say?

MOIRA

Remember Stella's post about Leon groping her at the last dance when she was in a floor-length gown?

CONNOR

Classic Leon.

MOIRA

What she was wearing would be allowed with this dress code.

SIMON

So then why does she care? Why do you care? You don't dress slutty.

MOIRA

Simon, don't say "slutty."

SIMON

Fine. You don't dress like a... revealingly.

MOIRA

The point is, it doesn't matter what we wear. Guys are gonna act like that anyway.

SIMON

Not all guys.

MOIRA

Yeah, but *some.*

CONNOR

Leon for sure.

MOIRA

So why are they making up rules for what girls can and can't wear? How come they aren't, like, talking to those guys about why that's not cool? How come when guys behave badly, girls get blamed?

SIMON
So this is, like, a feminist thing?

MOIRA
I think it's just a fairness thing.

CONNOR
Well, I'm in. If girls want to shake their booties in short shorts – they have my full support.

Beat.

What?

MOIRA
Okay. If we want to hit all the floors before first bell, we need to get moving. And Connor, you can't skip English, you have to go so you can walk out. That's the whole point.

CONNOR
Cool. I mean, if other people walk out. If I'm the only one, that's gonna be pretty awkward.

MOIRA
Guys, *please*, if my own friends aren't gonna walk out, that doesn't set the best example, does it?

CONNOR
Right. You're the mastermind.

MOIRA
Simon, you're in, right?

SIMON
Yeah. Of course.

MOIRA
You guys are amazing. Okay – let's go!

MOIRA exits, followed by CONNOR and SIMON.

AUDIO TRANSITION

> *AUDIO of a crowd cheering. MOIRA's voice cuts through the crowd.*

MOIRA's voice

We need to do more than police what girls wear. We need to have some honest conversations about whose behaviour is the problem!

> *A loud cheer from the crowd.*

MOIRA's voice

And I promise I won't stop until we've had that conversation, because OUR BODIES, OUR CLOTHES, STAND UP, BREAK OUR CODE!

> *The crowd joins in, chanting, "Break our code, break our code, break our code." Audio fades out.*

SCENE 4

> *SIMON enters, reviewing footage of Moira's speech on his phone. We hear audio of the tail end of her speech and the crowd's cheers. MOIRA enters in a state of joyful shock.*

SIMON
Hey there, revolutionary! Moi? You okay?

MOIRA
Was that not the most amazing thing ever??

SIMON
(*beginning to film*) Statement for the press, please!

MOIRA

Come on, put that away! Wait – you didn't film my speech, did you?

SIMON

Of course I did!

MOIRA

Simon!

SIMON

It was awesome! Come on, Moi, everybody was filming it! People were, like, all about you.

MOIRA

They did seem pretty into it, didn't they?

SIMON

Totally! I even saw Janice there.

MOIRA

Amazing!

SIMON

Yeah! What was the thing you said about the police?

MOIRA

What? Oh – "We need to do more than police what girls wear!"

SIMON

Yes! Boom – mic drop! When you said that, Janice cheered her head off.

MOIRA

Seriously?

SIMON

Yeah!

The bell rings.

MOIRA
Okay, I gotta get to chem. See you at lunch?

SIMON
Course!

MOIRA
'Kay.

> *MOIRA turns to go, then turns back and gives
> SIMON a hug.*

MOIRA
Thank you so much, Simon. You're the best.

> *MOIRA exits. SIMON basks in it all for a moment
> before exiting opposite.*

SCENE 5

> *MOIRA enters, unwraps a sandwich, and is about to
> take a bite when SIMON enters.*

SIMON
¡Hola!

MOIRA
¡Hola!

SIMON
What is that? Tuna?

MOIRA
Affirmative.

SIMON
Throw it out!

SIMON snatches the sandwich out of MOIRA's hand and throws it on the ground.

MOIRA
Hey! Simon, what is wrong with you?! That is such a waste of food!

MOIRA picks up the sandwich and throws it away.

SIMON
No lowly tuna for my political genius... Voila!

SIMON produces a bag of barbecue chips.

MOIRA
Barbecue?

SIMON
And...

SIMON produces salt and vinegar chips.

MOIRA
Salt and vinegar?!

SIMON
Annnnnnnnnnd...

SIMON produces ketchup chips.

MOIRA
Ketchup! The king of the chips!

SIMON
It's annnnnn...

MOIRA and SIMON
(*dancing and chanting*) All-chip lunch! All-chip lunch! All-chip lunch! All-chip –

CONNOR enters, yelling over them.

CONNOR
What the hell, Moira?

MOIRA
What?

CONNOR
You're supposed to *plan* dances, not get them cancelled!

MOIRA
Cancelled?

SIMON
Wait, what?

CONNOR
You haven't seen?

MOIRA
Seen what?

CONNOR
(*handing MOIRA a flyer*) They're handing them out outside the office.

MOIRA
I didn't go by the office.

    MOIRA scans the flyer.

SIMON
Me neither.

CONNOR
Well, I guess you're not the only one who can hand out flyers.

MOIRA
(*reading the flyer*) "Based on concerns expressed at this morning's demonstration, it is now the opinion of this administration that policies regarding *both* clothing and

student conduct are required to ensure that dances are fun, respectful, and safe. As these policies have not yet been determined, this year's spring dance will no longer take place."

SIMON
What?!

CONNOR
Yeah. "Stand up, break our code! Stand up, break our code!" Congratulations, Moi. Code's officially broken – can't have a dress code without a dance.

MOIRA
Oh my God!

CONNOR
The whole protest thing was such a stupid idea. "Break our code," what's that even supposed to mean?

MOIRA
It means the dress code wasn't fair! I meant what I said, if they want to change the way guys behave at dances they should be talking to the *guys*.

CONNOR
Yeah, rah, rah, rah – you're a real politician now. Especially the part where you piss everyone off.

SIMON
Woah – people aren't gonna be pissed at Moi, she was trying to do the right thing.

CONNOR
You're right, they're not *gonna* be pissed at Moi. They *are* pissed. Present tense. Hello, have you checked your phone?

MOIRA
No...

CONNOR
Well, your hashtag's blowing up. And not in a good way.

MOIRA pulls out her phone. She reads.

MOIRA
"When did @MagicMoi forget her job was to plan parties,
not be an uppity bitch? #BreakOurCode."

SIMON pulls out his phone and reads.

SIMON
"Guess @MagicMoi had a pretty slutty outfit planned.
Looks like someone's tired of being ignored. #SheThirsty
#BreakOurCode."

MOIRA
Wait, so yesterday I make up the dress code cuz I'm a
prude, and today I protest it cuz I'm easy? That doesn't even
make sense!

CONNOR
People are mad, Moi. You can't blame them. I mean, what did
you think would happen?

MOIRA
I don't know!

CONNOR
Yeah, well maybe you should have thought it through for,
like, five minutes, instead of running the whole school full
speed into a disaster.

MOIRA
I'm sorry, okay?

CONNOR

Whatever. I'm outta here.

CONNOR exits.

MOIRA

God, Connor can be such a jerk!

SIMON

He's just being Connor. He'll get over it.

MOIRA

What about everyone else?

SIMON

They will, too.

MOIRA

Yeah, right. I'm so stupid.

SIMON

Don't say that.

MOIRA

The protest ruined everything!

SIMON

C'mon, what were you supposed to do? People were screaming at you online to do something… You did something –

MOIRA

And it totally backfired!

SIMON

Okay, enough! C'mere. (*pulling MOIRA into a hug*) No more doom and gloom. Let's focus on the positive.

MOIRA

Where is there a positive here?

SIMON

Well... What do you want to do instead?

MOIRA

Instead of what?

SIMON

Instead of go to the dance together? We still have the limo...
Y'know, this could be even better!

MOIRA

Huh?

SIMON

Well, now we don't have to rush through dinner to get to the
dance where, no matter what I do, you're gonna be running
around, stressed about how it's going... We can just, like,
have dinner like we planned, get the limo to pick us up from
there and then... whatever. We could drive through the park,
or... or out the Point...

MOIRA

What are we gonna do at the Point?

SIMON

I mean, y'know... whatever.

MOIRA

That's, like, a make-out spot.

SIMON

Okay, well, where would you want to go?

MOIRA

Wait... were you picturing this like... was this supposed to be
a date?

SIMON

Um...

MOIRA
Oh.

SIMON
What did you think it was?

MOIRA
I guess I just thought we were going as friends.

SIMON
Of course.

MOIRA
I'm sorry.

SIMON
Right. I gotta go.

SIMON starts gathering his things.

MOIRA
Do you want to talk about this?

SIMON
No, I think I'm about as embarrassed as I need to be right now, thanks.

MOIRA
You shouldn't be! It was just a misunderstanding.

SIMON
Right. Yeah, I guess I misunderstood when you said, "It's a date."

MOIRA
I... It's an expression.

SIMON
Yeah, right.

MOIRA

Simon…

SIMON

Just forget it.

MOIRA

I honestly didn't know that's how you felt.

SIMON

Really? I spend about a hundred hours watching that stupid murder show with you, I memorize your favourite fricken' foods – you honestly saying none of that means anything?

MOIRA

Yeah, it means we're friends!

SIMON

God, what a waste of time.

MOIRA

Glad to hear that's how you feel about our friendship.

SIMON

How am I supposed to feel, Moi? All the time, you're, like, texting me 24-7… little random emojis and selfies. Don't act like that's not flirting!

MOIRA

I send emojis to everybody! That's just who I am.

SIMON

Yeah – a tease.

MOIRA

What?

> *Beat.*

SIMON and MOIRA stare at each other in stormy silence before SIMON shrugs and exits. Then MOIRA hastily gathers her stuff and exits.

AUDIO TRANSITION

Audio of Moira's voice cut together from her speech. Line breaks denote where the audio has been cut to skew her message.

Let's talk about this dress code.

We need

it

because of

people

like me.

I like

distracting

and

tempting.

I like the way it

feels.

It is not fair

to blame

literally half the student body

for

my

bad behaviour.

We need

this dress code

for

people

like

me. Because

I promise I won't stop

distracting or tempting.

I like the way it

feels.

SCENE 6

CONNOR enters, watching a video of Moira's cut-up speech on his phone. SIMON enters, catching the tail end of the audio.

SIMON
Bro.

CONNOR
Brosef. You seen Moira?

SIMON
No.

CONNOR
(*indicating his phone*) Are we gonna talk about this?

SIMON
What?

CONNOR
(*mocking him*) Yeah, "what." The video, dude.

SIMON
Of Moira?

CONNOR
Yeah, the one of Moira's speech, all cut up to make it say the opposite of what she meant?

SIMON
Yeah, I saw it.

CONNOR
And?

SIMON
And... what?

CONNOR
I'm just surprised – someone takes a shot like that at the love of your life, and you have no opinion?

SIMON
It's just someone's idea of a joke.

CONNOR
Pretty harsh joke.

SIMON
Yeah, well, people are pretty mad at her right now. You lost it on her yesterday.

CONNOR
Yeah, but I didn't make a cinematic tribute about it.

SIMON

Okay, so?

CONNOR

So it just seems a little over the top.

SIMON

Well, I don't know what to tell you. Some people are dramatic.

CONNOR

Pathetic, if you ask me.

SIMON

This coming from the guy who staked out a volleyball team to try to get some action.

CONNOR

At least I own my shit. Whoever put this out is too much of a coward to put their name on it. They made an anonymous account just to post it.

SIMON

Right.

CONNOR

Like I said, pathetic.

SIMON

You talk to her at all?

CONNOR

I texted her, like, a thousand times last night to see if she was okay – I even called her. No answer.

SIMON

Right.

CONNOR
So you haven't talked to her?

SIMON
Not since yesterday. We uh, we kinda had a fight.

CONNOR
'Bout what?

SIMON
She never wanted to go to the dance with me. Not like that.
She thought we were going as friends.

CONNOR
Damn.

SIMON
Yeah.

CONNOR
Sorry, dude.

SIMON
Whatever, right?

CONNOR
So that's why you did it?

SIMON
What?

CONNOR
You seriously gonna sit here and try to tell me you didn't
make that video?

SIMON
I don't know what // you're talking about.

CONNOR
You looking to mess up two friendships today? Don't
lie to me.

SIMON
Seriously. // I didn't.

CONNOR
Dude. I've known you since you had a *Finding Nemo* night
light. You've always sucked at lying.

SIMON
I'm not // lying.

CONNOR
Just –! Head to second six in the video.

> *SIMON plays through six seconds of the video
> and stops it.*

CONNOR
Bottom corner of the frame, dude. That's my hat. You were
standing behind me at the protest, I remember. You took this.

SIMON
No, I –

CONNOR
Simon.

SIMON
I didn't –

CONNOR
Stop it.

SIMON
Okay, so I took it. It's just a joke.

CONNOR
Yeah, I'm sure that's exactly how Moira sees it.

SIMON
Does she know it was me?

CONNOR
Like I said – haven't talked to her.

SIMON
Right.

CONNOR
But either way – you have to tell her.

SIMON
No, I don't!

CONNOR
I'm not gonna lie about this.

SIMON
Dude, whose side are you on? We're best friends.

CONNOR
Yeah, we are. All three of us.

SIMON
I'm talking about you and me. Guy code, dude. Bros
before hoes.

CONNOR
Did you get a brain transplant yesterday? Who am I even
talking to? Cuz the guy I know wouldn't sit here and call our
other best friend a "ho."

SIMON
You know what I mean.

CONNOR
Yeah, I think I do. I think you're saying that I should stick up for you, even though you're being an asshole, just because you and I both have Y chromosomes.

SIMON
...

CONNOR
You got burned. Sorry, bro. Doesn't give you a licence to do what you did.

SIMON
It's gonna blow over, okay? I took it down.

CONNOR
Yeah, after everyone in our grade already shared it! People saved it, Simon. They're sharing that. And we haven't even gotten into all the recuts.

SIMON
What recuts?

CONNOR
You haven't seen?

SIMON
No, I... I've kinda been staying offline since it took off. It kinda freaked me out.

CONNOR
Go to Leon's feed.

> *SIMON pulls out his phone and watches a video as we hear audio of Moira's voice saying phrases from the video: "I like the way it feels," "bad behaviour," "won't stop," etc. – cut together with pornographic sighs.*

SIMON
Woah.

CONNOR
Yeah. It's out of control.

SIMON
Well, I didn't think people were gonna do that!

CONNOR
What, is this your first day on the internet?

SIMON
You were mad about the dress code, too!

CONNOR
Yeah – so I yelled at her and went and got a Blizzard®! Learn to cope, dude.

SIMON
This is different! She totally led me on. Like we talked about. She was flirting.

CONNOR
Okay, so we got it wrong.

SIMON
No, look at this. (*scrolling through his phone, showing CONNOR*) A selfie in bio, "Bored as hell, rescue meeeeeeeee." A selfie while she's waiting for the bus… Selfie with her cat… My entire text feed with her is just emojis and selfies. Look! "Nap is life, life is nap" – she's in bed in this one! What the hell does she think selfies in bed mean?

CONNOR
It's not like they're nudes.

SIMON
Still – does she send you a thousand selfies?

CONNOR
She sends me some –

SIMON
From bed?

CONNOR
I don't know! I'm not paying as much attention as you.

SIMON
Well, did she send you this one?

CONNOR
I don't know.

SIMON
I bet she didn't. You would remember.

CONNOR
Maybe.

SIMON
You would remember, cuz you'd be, like, omigod, Moira just sent me a selfie in bed, what does this mean?

CONNOR
Probably not, dude! I don't see her that way.

SIMON
Whatever. Can you just admit I'm not crazy for thinking she was into me?

CONNOR
You're not crazy, you're just wrong.

SIMON
Yeah, but I'm wrong because of the way *she* acted.

CONNOR
I don't know, dude. I don't know if she led you on. But I do know posting that video crossed a line.

SIMON
So what, are you gonna tell her?

CONNOR
Like I said, *you* need to tell her.

SIMON
And if I don't? You gonna rat me out?

MOIRA enters. She sees CONNOR and SIMON.

MOIRA
Perfect.

MOIRA turns to leave.

CONNOR
Moi! Where you going?

MOIRA
Look, I just wanted some time to myself before class, I don't
really want to get yelled at right now.

CONNOR
No one's yelling! Did you get my texts? I was worried
about you.

MOIRA
I thought you were mad at me.

CONNOR
Look, I was mad for, like, an hour. But I shouldn't have been.
I acted like an idiot. I'm sorry, Moi. I was texting you cuz I
wanted to know if you were okay.

MOIRA
I'm fine.

CONNOR
You sure?

MOIRA

Is this it now? Is this my life?

CONNOR

What do you mean?

MOIRA

Like, until we graduate am I just video girl? Or what about after? This stuff follows you around. My cousin had a video about her, she changed schools and everything, it didn't matter, people knew! And they were horrible! She finished high school by correspondence! Is that gonna be me?

CONNOR

No!

MOIRA

(*breaking down*) I just don't understand how someone could hate me this much.

SIMON

Come on Moi, don't take it so personally. It's just a joke.

MOIRA

You think this is funny?!

SIMON

No! I just think that's what it was supposed to be.

MOIRA

It's only a joke if you currently hate me. All those recuts of the video? They're definitely not laughing *with* me, are they, Simon? They're mean, they're awful. Some of them are scary.

SIMON

I haven't really looked at them.

MOIRA

Well, you must be the only person at this school who hasn't. I had to turn my phone off last night, it just wouldn't stop.

SIMON
I'm sorry.

MOIRA
My mom is out for blood. She wants whoever it was expelled.

CONNOR
Seriously?

MOIRA
Yeah, she's meeting with the principal this afternoon. She wants to launch, like, a full-on investigation.

SIMON
Do you think that'll help? I mean – won't it make you an even bigger target?

MOIRA
It doesn't matter what I think, my mom is insisting. She said a stupid school dance is no reason to ruin someone's entire life.

CONNOR
Right.

A look passes between CONNOR and SIMON.

SIMON
Moi – can we talk?

MOIRA
Sure.

SIMON
Connor, can you give us a minute?

CONNOR
One hundred.

CONNOR starts to leave.

(*to MOIRA*) You need anything, shoot a text.

MOIRA
'Kay.

CONNOR rushes out, forgetting his backpack.

SIMON
Look – I'm sorry about yesterday. I was a dick.

MOIRA
Yeah, you were.

SIMON
I... yeah.

MOIRA
(*pause*) It's okay. I mean – I get it. I'm sorry I hurt your feelings.

SIMON
Don't worry about that.

MOIRA
So we're cool?

SIMON
I hope so.

MOIRA
Good. Cuz if every day is gonna be like right now is – I need all my friends.

SIMON
It's bad, hey?

MOIRA
It's... (*breaking down*) This is the worst day of my life.

SIMON

Oh, Moi – I'm so sorry... You want a hug?

MOIRA nods. MOIRA and SIMON hug. CONNOR enters to retrieve his backpack and is surprised and relieved to see them hugging.

CONNOR

Sorry, forgot my... whoa. You guys... good?

MOIRA

(*composing herself*) We're good, we're good.

CONNOR

Thank God. If I was gonna have to pick a side, I was gonna lose my mind.

MOIRA

Obviously, it would never come to that.

CONNOR

Totally! I mean, we can do damage control – he took the video down, so –

MOIRA

What?

CONNOR

What?

MOIRA

What are you talking about?

CONNOR

The... I'm talking about... What were you talking about?

SIMON

We were talking about yesterday. I told you, we had a fight? Things got a little out of hand?

CONNOR
Right, but –

MOIRA
(*to CONNOR*) Why are you talking about the video?

Beat.

(*to SIMON*) Simon, what is he talking about?

Beat. There's nothing else for SIMON to do.

SIMON
I… It was me.

Beat.

MOIRA
What?

SIMON
The video. I did it.

MOIRA
Why?

SIMON
Y'know, we had that fight, and I was mad, and… And I posted it.

MOIRA
…

SIMON
Look, I know it feels like it right now, but – it's not that bad, okay?

MOIRA
Not that –

SIMON

I mean, it's gonna blow over.

MOIRA

How could you do that?

SIMON

Because... I like you, okay? And I'm sorry, but you can't just string someone along and not expect them to be upset about it.

MOIRA

Simon, I have never strung you along –

SIMON

Oh, here we go again.

MOIRA

Yep! Here we go. Let's go. Let's do this. I don't know what I did to make you think I had feelings for you, but it was an accident. I know that sucks to hear, but that's what it was.

SIMON

Yeah, you just *accidentally* agreed to go on a date with me?

MOIRA

I didn't know that's what I was doing!

SIMON

You literally said the words "It's a date"!

MOIRA

Okay, Simon. Sure. Let the record show, Moira Schwartz said the well-accepted turn of phrase "It's a date!" She deserved everything she got after that!

SIMON

(*to CONNOR*) Connor, you know what I mean, right? She was flirting with me!

CONNOR

(*to MOIRA*) I said I didn't know!

MOIRA

Leave him out of this.

SIMON

Look, I am *trying* to apologize.

MOIRA

Well, you're doing a bang-up job.

SIMON

I took it down, Moi! What else can I do? It's gone, okay?

MOIRA

Gone?! It'll *never* be GONE, Simon. People saved it! They're recutting it and sending out things that are a thousand times worse!

SIMON

'Kay, but that has nothing to do with me.

MOIRA

Are you on glue? None of this would be happening without *your* video!

SIMON

People were posting stuff about you before I put the video out.

MOIRA

Not like this. Not recutting your video and looping me saying "I want it" over and over again, saying they're gonna do a bunch of gross stuff to me, whether I want it or not. Some of these are threats, Simon. My mom wants me to talk to the police about it.

SIMON
'Kay, that seems a little over the top.

MOIRA
Oh really?

MOIRA pulls out her phone and reads.

"I can't tell if @MagicMoi is the kind of girl who needs to get laid or smacked. Either way, sign me up."

SIMON
Okay, I get it.

MOIRA
Oh, I'm sorry, am I making you uncomfortable?

SIMON
Just – you don't need to read them out loud to me, okay?

MOIRA
You don't like it when I read them? Fine. *You* read them. Here's a good one.

MOIRA hands her phone to SIMON.

MOIRA
Read it.

CONNOR
C'mon, Moi, I think he gets it –

MOIRA
(*still to SIMON*) Read.

SIMON
I...

MOIRA
Simon!

SIMON swallows. He looks down at the phone.

SIMON
I... I'm not saying that.

MOIRA
Why? Aren't you proud?

SIMON
Proud of what? I didn't say that!

MOIRA
These are your fans, Simon. Your first video, out in the world, going viral – lucky you!

SIMON
I was mad, okay?

MOIRA
Okay, well I'm mad now, Simon! I'm mad! So what do I get to do? Do I get to make a video about how *you're* the thirsty one? How this all happened because *you* wanted *me* and I wasn't interested?

SIMON
Moira –

MOIRA
Or maybe other stuff? All bets are off, hey? This friendship's over, right? It was a "waste of time," right? So maybe anything you told me while you were my fake best friend is up for grabs, hey? Like about how much your mom drinks –

SIMON
Stop it.

MOIRA
Or how you had heart surgery when you were a kid and you still have nightmares about dying –

CONNOR
Moira –

MOIRA
I'm just trying to keep up, Connor! I'm just trying to be on his level.

SIMON
Yeah, there's such a thing as too far!

MOIRA
Yeah! There is! And you went there! You think I care in the long run if Leon fires off a quick post about how much I suck for getting the dance cancelled? Whatever. Leon's a dick.

But you... You were my best friend.

SIMON
I... I'm sorry, Moi. I was mad, and I wasn't thinking, and I messed things up. I wish I could take it back. I mean it.

MOIRA
...

SIMON
Moira, please. I'm so sorry. C'mon, I don't want things to be bad between us. I want things to be okay.

MOIRA
If you could make that video... We never were okay.

SIMON
I'll do anything, Moi. I'm really sorry, I mean it.

MOIRA
...

SIMON
Just tell me what to do.

MOIRA
Go away.

SIMON
Moi?

MOIRA
Turn around, walk away, and don't look back. Ever.

SIMON looks at CONNOR, who gives him nothing.
SIMON exits.

Beat.

CONNOR
Are you okay?

MOIRA
(*losing it*) I'm really, really not.

CONNOR
It's okay. It's gonna be okay.

MOIRA
How could he do that?

CONNOR
I don't know.

MOIRA
Do you think... Do you think I deserved it?

CONNOR
No! No way, Moi.

MOIRA
But what he said – about the flirting, do you think?

CONNOR
Who cares? You didn't want to go out with him. You're allowed to not want to go out with him.

MOIRA
Everybody hates me.

CONNOR
Everybody's stupid, and they get whipped up over anything.

MOIRA
When people find out it was Simon, they're going to have a field day.

CONNOR
Maybe nobody will figure it out.

MOIRA
They will. Someone will. And when they do –

CONNOR
We'll deal with it. It's not gonna last forever. Someone else will do something stupid, and people will get obsessed with that.

MOIRA
I guess.

CONNOR
Hey, maybe it'll be me.

MOIRA
That'd be good, if you could do that.

CONNOR
Give me a day. C'mon, let's get out of here. You wanna come over? You could catch me up on *Murder, She Wrote*?

MOIRA
We have class.

CONNOR

Class will be there tomorrow. You really want to go in there today?

CONNOR stands to leave. MOIRA doesn't.

CONNOR

You coming?

MOIRA

I can't run from this. Class will be there tomorrow, and so will everyone else. Might as well rip the Band-Aid off.

CONNOR

I guess.

MOIRA

I'm gonna go in.

CONNOR

You want company?

MOIRA

That would be nice.

CONNOR and MOIRA start to go. MOIRA stops.

MOIRA

This is gonna sound weird, but... You know we're just friends, right?

CONNOR

Of course. Best friends.

MOIRA

'Kay. Let's go.

MOIRA and CONNOR exit.

THE END

Acknowledgments

First and foremost, I must thank Patrick McDonald, the former artistic director of Green Thumb Theatre and the original director of the premiere productions of both *Still • Falling* and *The Code*, for his guidance, insight, and encouragement. I sent Patrick a very long and unfocused script called "Untitled Teen Depression Project" in the fall of 2013, and he saw enough potential in the idea and in me to commission what became *Still • Falling*. Without Patrick, neither of these plays would exist. I am forever grateful to him for his belief in me and in the importance of work for and about young people.

I must also thank Shawn Macdonald, who I originally sent that very rough script to, and who encouraged me to share it with Patrick.

Thank you to all of the incredible artists who have inhabited these characters, both in production and in various stages of development: Caitlin McCarthy, Gili Roskies, Olivia Hutt, Lisa Baran, David Sklar, Evelyn Chew, Mike Payette, Elizabeth Barrett, Mason Temple, Nathan Kay, Joe Rose, Teo Saefkow, Isaac Li, and Matthew Rhodes. Thank you to the Banff Playwrights Lab and to Jenna Rodgers and Brian Quirt for their support in the development of *The Code*.

Thank you to Green Thumb Theatre staff, past and present, for all of the work you have done to bring my work to young people across North America.

Thank you, Joan MacLeod, for the incredibly kind words at the beginning of this book and for being an inspiration and a shining example to Canadian playwrights.

Thank you to my family – my parents, Kathryn and Stephen, brother and sister-in-law Ben and Erin, and my love, my husband Kyle – thank you for believing in me, for supporting me, and, more than anything, for loving me.

And to my daughter, Elliot Eva – thank you for letting me be your Mama. It is the best job in the world.

Talonbooks would like to thank Green Thumb Theatre for their kind permission to reprint edited versions of their study guides.

Rachel Aberle is a theatre artist born and raised in various parts of Greater Vancouver, on areas including the Traditional, Ancestral, and unceded Territories of the xʷməθkʷəy̓əm (Musqueam), Sḵwx̱wú7mesh, səl̓ilwətaʔɬ (Tsleil-Waututh), Stó:lō, sc̓əwaθən məsteyəxʷ (Tsawwassen), Stz'uminus, Qayqayt, q̓ic̓əy̓ (Katzie), kʷikʷəƛ̓əm (Kwikwetlem), and q̓ʷa:n̓ƛ̓ən̓ (Kwantlen) Nations. As a playwright, Rachel strives to explore complex issues with humour and curiosity. Her first play, *Still • Falling*, has toured across North America and received the Jessie Richardson Theatre Award for Significant Artistic Achievement. Her second play, *The Code*, was recognized with the Sydney J. Risk Prize for Outstanding Original Script by an Emerging Writer. Rachel is the artistic director of Green Thumb Theatre and a graduate of Studio 58. Her greatest joy in life is being a mom to the one and only Elliot Eva, who inspires, surprises, and challenges her every single day.

PHOTO CREDIT: Erin Aberle-Palm

GREEN THUMB
THEATRE

STILL · FALLING

By Rachel Aberle

STUDY
GUIDE

Supported by

Canada Council   Conseil des arts
for the Arts   du Canada

BRITISH COLUMBIA
ARTS COUNCIL
An agency of the Province of British Columbia

BRITISH
COLUMBIA
Supported by the Province of British Columbia

CITY OF
VANCOUVER

RBC Foundation
RBC Fondation

ACTUALIZE8

Green Thumb Theatre operates on the Lands of the Coast
Salish Peoples, including the unceded Territories of the
xʷməθkʷəy̓əm (Musqueam), Sḵwx̱wú7mesh (Squamish),
and səl̓ilwətaʔɬ (Tsleil-Waututh) Nations.

Anxiety BC (now Anxiety Canada) reviewed and approved the content in this
study guide relating to anxiety. See www.anxietycanada.com.

Production photos of Olivia Hutt by
Moonrider Productions

WWW.GREENTHUMB.BC.CA

TABLE OF CONTENTS

ABOUT ANXIETY AND DEPRESSION

Anxiety affects our thoughts, body, and behaviours. It is:
- Our body's reaction to perceived danger or important events
- Something that everyone experiences from time to time

Too much anxiety can:
- Prevent you from engaging in age-appropriate activities
- Prevent you from meeting expected developmental milestones

Common examples of interference and disruption include:
- Academic failure
- Keeping isolated or failing to join in and make friends
- Refusing to go on school field trips
- Resisting participating in new activities or trying new things
- School refusal

> *"It started as anxiety, it moved to full depression… I started to disengage from friends, family, society in general …"*
>
> www.cbc.ca/news/canada/british-columbia/age-of-anxiety-panel-1.3255344

Depression is a mood disorder that causes a persistent feeling of sadness and loss of interest. Also called major depressive disorder or clinical depression, it affects how you feel, think, and behave and can lead to a variety of emotional and physical symptoms. Just like anxiety, some sadness or occasional feelings of being depressed are normal. Feeling depressed once in a while does not mean that you have major depression.

> Self-injury, or self-harm, is the deliberate and direct destruction of one's body tissue without suicidal intent.

SYNOPSIS

Nina (or Nick in the second version of the play) has a great life. She loves her family, she does well in school, and her friends are awesome. But suddenly Nina starts feeling … off, and she finds herself slipping into a dark reality she cannot understand, let alone articulate to the people around her. *Still • Falling* follows Nina as she tries to come to terms with what it means to struggle with anxiety and depression, and to rise above it with as much strength, and as few scars, as possible. A realistic, honest, and bitingly funny look at the difference between "teen angst" and mental illness and the ways vulnerable kids can start to find their way out of the dark.

CONTENT ADVISORY

The content of this play may make for an intense experience for some viewers. The main character's portrayal is an honest, open, and candid representation of a teen with anxiety and depression and displaying non-suicidal self-harm. It is advised that all teachers, school counsellors, school psychologists, and administration be informed about the nature of this play and be aware that some scenes may be emotionally triggering to some students. It is also advised that students should be made aware of the play's themes prior to viewing.

The pre- and post-performance discussion questions and exercises will be valuable support for students' immediate and long-term well-being and self-care. It is strongly recommended that teachers allot some class time for students to discuss the play's themes and topics after viewing, either informally or formally with the exercises and activities provided in this guide.

Schools should be ready to deal with various reactions and questions from their students. It is our hope that this play will encourage youth in crisis to reach out for help, and therefore teachers, counsellors, and in-school mental-health teams should be prepared to debrief and deal with possible disclosures from at-risk students in the days and weeks following the performance.

WHY THIS PLAY?

Green Thumb Theatre chose to produce *Still • Falling* to encourage conversation and awareness and to help students gain a deeper understanding of mental health and especially how it can affect them and their peers. Green Thumb Theatre creates and produces plays that explore social issues relevant to the lives of children, youth, and young adults. We provide theatre that celebrates the language and stories of today's generation and culture to stimulate empathy, debate, and critical thinking. As with all of our plays, we challenge our audiences to re-examine their beliefs and prejudices and to define their feelings and aspirations.

HOW TO USE THIS GUIDE

Green Thumb recognizes how important discussions around mental health are in order to destigmatize mental illness and engage youth in conversations about their own mental health and self-care. Green Thumb also recognizes and values the role that teachers play in positively influencing youth development, and how teachers can be front-line interveners and supports to youth who may be struggling with mental-health concerns.

To create this educational guide, mental-health professionals and teachers were consulted and information from websites providing current, credible, and respected mental-health and educational, peer-reviewed research was used. Subject areas are explored that may inspire viewers, while furthering knowledge and facilitating dialogue about mental health after watching the production of *Still • Falling*.

The British Columbia Ministry of Education curriculum was analyzed to ensure the following exercises could be utilized to address Grade 8–12 Core Competencies/Content in the areas of Planning, Arts Education – Visual Arts, English Language Arts – Creative Writing, Communications – Media Arts, Health Leadership, and Physical and Health Education. British Columbia's curriculum has been redesigned to respond to the demanding world students are entering. As well as Essential Learning, Literacy, and Numeracy Foundations, the Ministry of Education has identified Communication and Thinking, plus Personal and Social Competencies students will need to develop for successes in the future. *Still • Falling* specifically addresses these by offering opportunities to:

* Analyze strategies for promoting mental well-being, for self and others
* Assess and evaluate strategies for managing problems related to mental well-being and substance use, for self and others
* Create and evaluate strategies for managing physical, emotional, and social changes during puberty and adolescence
* Take creative risks to experience and express thoughts, emotions, ideas, and meaning
* Construct meaningful personal connections between self, text, and world
* Understand and care about themselves and others, and to find and achieve their purposes in the world
* Assess how prevailing conditions and the actions of individuals and groups affect events, decisions, and developments (cause and consequence).

—**Cathryn McPhee**, M.Ed. in Health Education and Active Living
Study Guide author

A NOTE FROM THE PLAYWRIGHT

Being a teenager is hard. Your body is changing, your hormones are all over the map – and this affects your mood. It can make what could seem like a small crisis to someone else seem like the end of the world to you. It can make you angry. It can make you sad. It can make you anxious.

These are all statements that are true to a degree, and all statements I heard a number of times when I was a teenager. I heard some version of these statements from my parents, from my teachers. My friends and I repeated these phrases to each other, as well, in times of stress. I repeated these phrases to myself, increasingly, as my mood went from bad to worse over my grade-twelve year. I blamed my age bracket for my increasing anxiety and sadness, trying to chalk up the emotional turmoil I was dealing with to a typical teenage phase.

By the time I received help, I was at a point of crisis. It took me a long time to ask for help with my mental health, and even longer for people to really hear me when I asked. Conversations around mental health were nowhere near as common as they are today. People – including myself – were much quicker to jump to the narrative of a typical teenage fluctuation in hormones than to dig deeper and question whether what was happening to me might require more attention and more targeted help.

My intent in creating this piece was to normalize conversations around mental health, to offer avenues for youth and young adults to connect with one another on the topic, and to encourage conversation with the adults in their lives, as well. I hope that teenagers who see *Still • Falling* will take away that drowning in emotional distress is *not* what a normal teenage experience has to look like, and that they will learn to ask for help early and often if they are feeling overwhelmed. I hope, too, that both the students and educators who see *Still • Falling* will begin to look out for the kinds of signposts that can be indicators of mental illness. As we begin to acknowledge how common mental illness is, I hope that as a community we can begin to look out for each other and to create positive space for people who are struggling.

And to anyone out there who sees this play who is suffering, who has reached a point of crisis, or is close to reaching one, I hope this play can let you know that you are not alone. Ask for the help you need – it is out there, and it does make a difference. And as you embark on a path towards recovery, be patient with yourself. Be patient, and be kind.

—**Rachel Aberle**

TERMINOLOGY RELATED TO THE PLAY

ANXIETY – Anxiety is part of our internal warning system; it is the fear or worry and physical changes in our body that we experience when we feel something bad might be about to happen. Everyone feels anxious at times, but too much anxiety can interfere with school, work, home life, and relationships.

ANXIETY PROBLEM or ANXIETY DISORDER – Anxiety is normal, but it can become a problem when it becomes intense or continual and makes it harder for you to do the things you want to do. If it causes enough problems, it may be considered within a group of mental illnesses called anxiety disorders. Anxiety disorders can take many different forms; two of the most common forms are social anxiety and panic disorder. Anxiety disorders are very treatable.

COUNSELLING or THERAPY – It's useful to talk to someone about any problem; some people find that simply talking with friends or family can help them feel better. A mental-health professional can offer more: they have training, experience, and emotional distance (since they don't know you). They use different theories to listen to you and support you, and they have expertise to approach different problems or patterns to manage your distress.

DEPRESSION – Feeling sad or low from time to time is a part of life, but a persistent low mood could be a sign of depression. For some people, depression makes them irritable or causes them to act out against others. Depression becomes a problem when the feelings don't go away, or if they intensify or begin to interfere with school, work, family, and friends. Depression is also a treatable disorder. Sometimes people who develop depression may also have a history of anxiety disorder. There is no evidence that one disorder causes the other, but there is clear evidence that many people suffer from both disorders.

MENTAL HEALTH – Mental health is defined as a state of well-being in which every individual realizes their own potential, can cope with the normal stresses of life, can work productively and fruitfully, and is able to make a contribution to their community.

MENTAL ILLNESS – Mental illnesses can take many forms, just as physical illnesses do. They are characterized by alterations in thinking, mood, or behaviour associated with significant distress and impaired functioning.

PANIC ATTACK – A sudden rush of intense fear or discomfort, which includes at least four of the following symptoms: racing or pounding heart, sweating, shaking or trembling, shortness of breath or feelings of being smothered, feeling of choking, chest pain or discomfort, chills or hot flashes, nausea or upset stomach, dizziness or lightheadedness, a sense of things being unreal or feeling detached from oneself, numbness or tingling sensations, fear of losing control or "going crazy," and fear of dying. Panic attacks tend to start quickly and reach a peak within ten minutes. The peak generally lasts for about five to ten minutes before the symptoms start to settle; however, it can take quite some time for all the symptoms to subside.

PANIC DISORDER – People with panic disorder experience unexpected and repeated panic attacks. They can become terrified that they may have more attacks and fear that something bad will happen because of them (such as "going crazy," losing control, or dying).

SELF-CARE – Any intentional actions a person takes to care for their physical, mental, and emotional health.

SELF-HARM or SELF-INJURY – Self-injury means that someone hurts themself on purpose but doesn't intend to end their life. Common acts of self-injury include cutting skin and burning skin. Self-injury itself isn't a mental illness but may be a sign that someone needs care and support. People who self-injure are not trying to end their lives, but they can experience those thoughts. When they self-injure, they are trying to cope with difficult or overwhelming thoughts or feelings.

SOCIAL INCLUSION – This means a feeling of belonging, being valued and respected, and able to take part in your community and benefit equally from what it has to offer.

STIGMA – A set of negative and often unfair beliefs that a society or group of people have about something, and the shame that a person carries as a result of being associated with it.

STRESS – A state of mental or emotional strain or tension resulting from adverse or very demanding circumstances; a state of mental, emotional, or physical strain when the demands placed on you are more than you can cope with. Stressful events (or events that lead to stress) can be either positive, such as graduating and going to university, or negative, such as an illness in the family or feeling overwhelmed by homework and exams.

SUICIDE – The deliberate taking of one's own life is the second leading cause of death among young people in Canada. Suicide and motor-vehicle accidents account for almost 60 percent of youth deaths. This figure is not just relevant in Canada – globally, suicide is among the top three causes of death among young people (aged fifteen to thirty-four). Suicide itself is not a mental disorder, but one of the most important causes of suicide is mental illness.

SUICIDE IDEATION – Having thoughts about how to kill oneself, which can range from a detailed plan to a fleeting consideration and does not include the final act of killing oneself. The majority of people who experience suicide ideation do not carry it through.

Sources
www.anxietycanada.com/learn-about-anxiety/anxiety-in-youth/
www.heretohelp.bc.ca
www.cmha.ca/mental_health/youth-and-self-injury

PRE-PERFORMANCE DISCUSSION

1. How do you define mental illness?
2. When you picture someone who's mentally ill, what do you see?
3. What things at school or home are sources of stress/pressure?
4. Brainstorm some of the pressures of being a teenager.
5. How do students typically cope with these stresses?
6. Do you know of anyone who has experienced mental illness?

Suggested pre-performance videos

1. "Millie – Most likely to panic"
   www.youtube.com/watch?v=VRKcDAOILI4
2. "The Science of Depression"
   www.youtube.com/watch?v=GOK1tKFFIQI
3. "Mental Health Awareness"
   www.youtube.com/watch?v=_OzWt8zZ0rw

WHAT TO CONSIDER WHILE WATCHING

1. Is this portrayal reinforcing myths about mental illnesses, or does it address these myths or highlight a new way of understanding mental illness?
2. What is the difference between feeling blue and being depressed?
3. How would you want to be treated if you developed or were struggling with mental illness?
4. What does this statement mean to you: "There is no health without mental health."

POST-PERFORMANCE QUESTIONS

1. What kinds of support did Nina seek out for her mental-health problems, if any?
2. What do you think would have happened if Nina had let her parents or her friends know earlier how she was feeling and what she was experiencing?
3. How did Nina's family and friends respond to her mental health problems? Were they helpful?
4. If you were Nina's friend and she told you what was going on and how she was feeling, how would you respond?
5. Is anxiety a sign of weakness? Is depression? Define "courage."

ACTIVITIES & EXERCISES

ACTIVITY
MENTAL ILLNESS, TRUE OR FALSE?

Below are some common statements about mental illness and suicide. Read them aloud to your students and have them identify if they are true or false.

Mental illnesses aren't real illnesses.

FALSE – Mental illnesses create distress, don't go away on their own, and are real health problems for which effective treatments exist. When someone breaks their arm, we wouldn't expect them to just "get over it." Nor would we blame them if they needed a cast, sling, or other help in their daily life while they recovered.

Mental illnesses don't affect very many people.

FALSE – All of us will be affected by mental illnesses. Researchers estimate that as many as one in five Canadians will experience a mental illness at some point in their life. You may not experience a mental illness yourself, but it's very likely that a family member, friend, or co-worker will experience challenges.

Telling yourself to "relax" is a very effective way to deal with anxiety.

FALSE – When you struggle with anxiety, it's not as simple as just telling yourself to "relax." Most people have to learn some new coping strategies to help them better deal with anxiety. The good news is that there is help available.

If you have a mental illness, you will never recover.

FALSE – People can and do recover from mental illnesses. Today, there are many different kinds of treatments, services, and supports that can help. No one should expect to feel unwell forever. The fact is that people who experience mental illnesses can and do lead productive, engaged lives.

Half of all lifetime cases of mental illness begin by age fourteen.

TRUE – Mental-health illnesses are the most prevalent of all health issues among children, adolescents, and young adults, and are much more likely to disrupt young people's lives than physical ailments. Early identification and linking young people with resources to strengthen their mental health are key to reducing the burden of mental illnesses. As with any health issue, we are better equipped if we are able to recognize the signs and symptoms early. Early recognition and appropriate help-seeking can happen only if young people know about the early changes that may indicate a mental-health issue, the types of help available, and how to access this help.

Only "emos" self-harm; it's part of modern-day youth culture.

FALSE – There's no such thing as a typical person who self-harms. It can affect anyone of any age, background, or race, regardless of whether they are an extrovert or an introvert.

People who experience mental illnesses are weak and can't handle stress.

FALSE – Stress impacts well-being, but this is true for everyone. Sometimes people who have experienced mental illnesses may gain tools that aid them with managing stress. Many people who experience mental illnesses learn skills like stress management and problem-solving so they can take care of stress before it affects their well-being. Taking care of yourself and asking for help when you need it are signs of strength, not weakness.

Anxiety problems are common.

TRUE – Anxiety problems are the most common mental-health problem. In fact, approximately one in four teens will experience some type of problem with anxiety at some point. If you struggle with anxiety, you are not alone!

Kids can't have a mental illness like depression. That is an adult problem.

FALSE – Even children can experience mental illness. In fact, many mental illnesses first appear when a person is young. Mental illness may look different in children than in adults, but it is a real concern. Mental illness can impact the way young people learn and build skills, which can lead to challenges in the future. Unfortunately, many children don't receive the help they need.

People who attempt suicide are just looking for attention.

FALSE – A suicide attempt is often the critical event that leads a deeply distressed person to a first contact with a helping professional such as a physician or psychologist. An attempt at suicide is a desperate cry for help – it is not an action that should be classified as attention-seeking behaviour.

Talking to someone about whether or not they are suicidal will make their suicidal symptoms worse.

FALSE – Asking someone if they have thoughts of suicide will not put the idea in their head if they are not suicidal. If they are having suicidal thoughts, knowing that you are concerned enough about them to ask may give them the courage to ask for help.

Sources

www.cmha.ca/mental_health/myths-about-mental-illness/#.Vg7jr0udBuY
www.teenmentalhealth.org/learn/suicide/

ACTIVITY
WIPE OUT STIGMA

It is well recognized that teens and young adults resist seeking help due in part to misinformation and the stigma attached to mental illness. In this activity, have students research anxiety disorders and depression and then identify and dispel the myths still attached to these mental illnesses.

Create public awareness posters or graphics that debunk common myths about mental illness.

MATERIALS
- Markers, poster board, magazines, scissors
- An electronic device with internet access

Help students in your school understand depression and anxiety by getting together in small groups to create an eye-catching poster or graphic that tackles one of the myths discussed in class. To get information to back up the statements made on your poster, use the websites listed on the Resources page of this guide to research mental-illness facts: how common it is, what outcomes can come from seeking help early, the importance of creating a safe community where mental illness is not stigmatized, and so on.

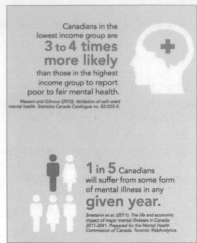

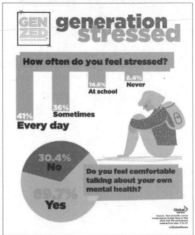

ACTIVITY
KNOW YOUR RIGHTS / MAKE YOUR RIGHTS

Create a Student Bill of Rights

The 1960 Canadian Bill of Rights and Freedoms was this country's first federal law to protect human rights and fundamental freedom. Considered groundbreaking at the time, it was eventually superseded by the 1982 Canadian Charter of Rights and Freedoms. Section 15 – Equality Rights makes it clear that every individual in Canada, regardless of race, religion, national or ethnic origin, colour, sex, age, or physical or mental disability, is to be considered equal. This means that governments must not discriminate on any of these grounds in their laws or programs.

See the Guide to the Canadian Charter of Rights and Freedoms: www.canada.ca/en/canadian-heritage/services/how-rights-protected/guide-canadian-charter-rights-freedoms.html.

With this Charter in mind, research and create a "Student Bill of Rights" for your school, making sure to include mental health. Brainstorm ideas on how to educate and promote tolerance, understanding, and acceptance in your school. Research has identified social inclusion to be one of the strongest determinants of mental health. How can you ensure basic rights are afforded to all students in your school community?

A sample of the Canadian Mental Health Association's Bill of Client Rights can be found at: camh.ca/en/your-care/your-rights/bill-of-client-rights.

EXERCISE
TAKE CHARGE: TAKING CARE OF YOURSELF

Using the resources at the end of this guide and the self-care guidelines on the next page, think about the following:

- **WHO?** Who in your community can you talk to and share how you are feeling?
- **WHERE?** What credible resources can you turn to?
- **WHAT?** What three self-care actions you can take to be good to yourself. These should be positive ways that you can cope or destress when you are having a tough time.

CLASSROOM DISCUSSION

1. Ask the students to spend a few minutes thinking about possible answers to fill in the grid below. Then have students brainstorm as a group options for all three columns.
2. Reflecting on Nina's situation, have the class brainstorm possible solutions that Nina could have used earlier to help her understand her emotions and reach out for help.
3. Have each student prepare their own personal "Take Charge Plan" with resources, people, and self-care activities. This would include individuals they trust and feel would support them during times of increased stress.

Who to go to for help three people you can trust	Where to go for help credible resources	Self-care three healthful things you can do to be good to yourself
1. Could be the name of a school counsellor or teacher	1.	1.
2.	2.	2.
3.	3.	3.

Feel free to add more resources and supports to this list. Check out the Wellness Modules at Here to Help, www.heretohelp.bc.ca/wellness-modules.

Remember, if self-care isn't working for you, and negative or anxious thoughts or emotions are starting to overwhelm you, the best way to cope with your feelings is to talk to someone.

PREVENTION

Mental health is not just the absence of mental illness. Positive mental health involves emotional and psychological wellness, healthy self-esteem and relationships, and an ability to take control of actions and feelings on a daily basis. By being aware, we can take positive steps towards mental health when the balance is disrupted.

TIPS FOR CONTROLLING STRESS

TALK ABOUT IT – Sharing your troubles with a friend may help you put things in perspective and not feel that you're alone. You may also learn some other ways to manage stress effectively.

HEALTHY DIET – A good diet is often the first thing to go when we're feeling stressed. Making a meal instead of buying one ready-made may seem like a challenge, but it will probably be cheaper and certainly be better for you, and the simple action of doing something good for yourself can soothe stressful feelings.

SLEEP – Getting a good night's sleep can reduce stress levels. We know that over time poor sleeping habits will wear down your body.

VISUALIZATION – Athletes achieve results by picturing themselves crossing the finish line first. Use the same technique to practise "seeing" yourself succeed in whatever situation is uppermost in your mind. See au.reachout .com/articles/how-to-challenge-negative-thoughts.

EXERCISE – You don't have to train for a marathon, but regular, moderate exercise helps ease tension and improves sleep and self-esteem. Making exercise a habit is key.

ENJOY YOURSELF – Taking the time for a favourite hobby is a great way of connecting with your creative self and nurturing it.

SET REALISTIC GOALS – Learning to say no is essential for some people. Assess your schedule and identify tasks or activities that you can or should let go of. Don't automatically volunteer to do something until you've considered whether it is feasible and healthy for you to do so.

LEARN RELAXATION TECHNIQUES – Practicing meditation or breathing awareness every day can relieve chronic stress and realign your outlook in a more positive way. Good breathing habits alone can improve both your psychological and physical well-being. See additional resources at au.reachout.com/mental-fitness/chilling-out.

VIDEO ON SELF-CARE AND COMPASSION
vimeo.com/groups/126256/videos/118911442

SELF-HELP EXERCISES
www.walkalong.ca/explore/self-help-exercises

EXERCISE
CHARACTER DEVELOPMENT

What would you do, what would you say?

Imagine that you are one of the characters in the play other than Nina/Nick. Whether you are the mother (Little Miss Sunshine/the Sunbeam), father (the Professor/the Coach), little brother (the Creep), or one of the friends (Kate, Ash, or Ian/Chris, Asher, or Nour), step into their character and continue to think about the friendship and relationship they have with Nina/ Nick. Then consider what would happen to your character if Nina/Nick had told you about how they were feeling and what they were experiencing. This could give you an opportunity to expand and develop your character.

Think about how you would do this and write a script or scenario narrating how you would respond.

- What would you say or not say?
- What would you do?
- Would your character change?
- Would you shut down?
- Would you reach out?
- How would you listen?
- Would you have something to share?

Mental illness doesn't discriminate and can affect people of any age or gender. Due to societal pressures to "stay strong" and "be tough," men often find seeking help with mental illness especially difficult.

Consider the following four suggestions while you are developing your character and your script.

FOUR KEY THINGS THAT CAN HELP YOU SUPPORT YOUR FRIEND

1.   **LOOK OUT FOR THE SIGNS** – Sometimes it can be hard to know if your friend is just going through a rough patch or whether there might be something more serious going on, like anxiety or depression. You might notice that they are not hanging out with their friends as much anymore or are always tired and feeling down. They might be snappier or perhaps look a mess. When you notice these changes, check in with your friend to see if they're okay.

2.   **LISTEN TO YOUR FRIEND'S EXPERIENCES** – Sitting and quietly listening is the next step. Don't rush to offer advice. Let them know you are there for them and that you want to help where you can. If they don't want to talk about it, respect that. Let them know you are worried and that you will be happy to listen when they want to talk, or suggest other people they might talk to. By listening and responding in a non-judgmental and reassuring manner, you are helping in a major way.

3.   **TALK ABOUT WHAT'S GOING ON** – Knowing what to say can sometimes be difficult. You might not be sure how to start a conversation with them, or you might be worried about saying the wrong thing. You could say things like, "I've noticed that you seem a bit down lately," or perhaps, "You seem like you are really down and not yourself; I really want to help you. Is there anything I can do?" Showing that you are willing to listen to what is going on can be very supportive for your friend. You don't need to have all the answers.

4.   **SEEK HELP TOGETHER** – Encourage your friend to get some support. They might want to start by talking with their family or a school counsellor about what has been going on, or they may prefer to talk with someone that they do not know, like a doctor or health professional. You could help them find a health professional and arrange an appointment with them; you might even offer to go with them to their first appointment to help them feel more relaxed about it. If they don't feel comfortable with the first health professional, encourage them to keep looking until they find one they do feel comfortable with.

See www.youthbeyondblue.com/help-someone-you-know /supporting-a-friend.

Most importantly, if at any time you are worried for your friend's safety, seek help. Talk to an adult about your concerns and ask for help in keeping your friend safe.

THINGS YOU CAN SAY TO A TEENAGER WITH ANXIETY OR DEPRESSION

- "No matter how bad things seem, I want you to know that I'm here for you."
- "Even if all I can give you is a shoulder to cry on, I want you to know you can count on it."
- "Depression and anxiety are illnesses. They can happen to anyone, and they're nothing to be ashamed of."
- "Asking for help doesn't make you weak, and it doesn't mean you've failed. It's one of the bravest things a person can do, and you should be proud of yourself."
- "I might not have any advice to give, but if you ever want to talk about what you're feeling, I promise I will listen."
- "I know everything feels really hard these days, so don't be afraid to tell me what you need."
- "You don't ever have to thank me for being here for you. I care about you, and it's my choice. It's what friends do."
- "Even though you don't feel like yourself these days, I want you to know that to me, you're still the same amazing person."
- "I may not be able to completely understand what's going on for you, because I haven't experienced it myself, but I'm here for you all the same."
- "I can't tell you how long you're going to feel this way, but I can tell you I plan on being here for you whenever you need me."

THINGS TO AVOID SAYING TO A TEENAGER WITH ANXIETY OR DEPRESSION

- "Snap out of it! Go have fun!"
- "You know, a lot of people in the world have it way worse than you do."
- "Stop pitying yourself so much."
- "Just remember, what you're feeling isn't really real. It's all in your head."
- "You have to stop playing the victim all the time."
- "I don't get it, you don't look sick."
- "Just try to look on the bright side more."
- "Get some rest and take some vitamins. That's what I do when I'm stressed, and it always works."
- "Come on, smile! Don't look so blue!"
- "You just need a girlfriend/boyfriend."
- "Whenever I feel down, I have a hot bath and I feel great again. Try that?"
- "You know, there are other ways to get attention."

See depressionteenshelp.com/teenagers-and-depression/.

ACTIVITY
A NOTE FROM A FRIEND

Responding to a Friend in Need

> I've been trying to figure out how to tell you, but it's embarrassing, so I keep putting it off. I started hurting myself again a few weeks ago. It makes me feel so ashamed and like there's something wrong with me ... I don't know why I do it. It's like I want to scream, but I don't want people to think I'm a freak, so instead I just do this because it's like it can just be my secret, you know? I don't want to do this anymore, but I don't know how to stop. Can we talk? All I know for sure is that something has to change.

When somebody has the courage to tell you that they self-harm, it is incredibly important to show them that you take them seriously, regardless of how severe, or not, the injury is. Your reaction may have a tremendous impact on them. Being available, whenever possible, to talk to a friend who self-harms can make all the difference, as feelings of isolation are often part of the problem. Let the person self-harming know that self-harm is very common and that individuals who do it are by no means alone.

In pairs, look at "A Note from a Friend." Consider what advice you would give to this person as a friend.

- What can you do that is helpful?
- What do you think would not be helpful?

Make sure that your friend knows who they can go to for expert help. Encourage your friend to seek help. If they are reluctant to tell other people, it's important to acknowledge that you aren't able to help them all on your own. If your friend is under eighteen years old, help should be from a trusted adult or mental-health professional.

Using the list of resources on pages 160 and 161, find three websites or phone numbers that provide useful, helpful information that you can share with your friend, so they realize they are not alone and there is help for them.

Be sure to take care of your own emotional well-being. Supporting a friend who self-injures can be difficult, so make sure that you also have some good supports in place and that your friend who self-injures knows who you may be talking to (for example, do not gossip or talk to other peers about your friend's self-injury without their permission). You may want to talk to a mental-health professional.

FOR TEACHERS
A NOTE FROM A FRIEND

Responding to a Friend in Need

After the student pairs have completed the "A Note from a Friend" exercise, provide an opportunity to discuss their responses and ensure the following feedback is highlighted:

- DO NOT tell the person what to do – allow them to have control over what they want to happen.
- DO NOT tell them to stop. Although this seems counterintuitive, stopping is very difficult and takes time and support – the person will first need to find other, safer ways of coping.
- DO offer to support them in seeking help if that is what they want.
- DO continue to be their friend.
- Seek help for yourself if you need support.
- Offer to listen to them and give them time and space to talk.
- Offer to help if they need it.

Do not allow students to share detailed information regarding self-harming. When educating youth about self-harming behaviour, discuss the behaviour in its broader context, that is, as a maladaptive coping strategy among several others (such as substance abuse or risk-taking). Educating students about signs of distress in themselves and others, as well as teaching the use of positive coping skills, is appropriate and recommended.

As a follow-up exercise, have each student brainstorm things they do when they are feeling low that help them feel better; then meet as a group and list each student's activities on a whiteboard for all students to see.

Additional educational supports for teachers can be found at:

www.cmha.ca/documents/youth-and-self-injury

www.heretohelp.bc.ca/infosheet/self-harm

When talking about the subject of self-harm, it is important to acknowledge that this could be a trigger for young people who are currently self-harming or have self-harmed in the past. Be aware of any students that may be affected and make sure support is outlined and highlighted.

Sources

www.samaritans.org/how-we-can-help/schools

sioutreach.org/learn-self-injury/

ACTIVITY
CHANNELLING EMOTION: MAKING POEMS OUT OF FEELINGS

Writing poems can be a cathartic emotional release; through a writing process, students may tap into their emotions and express them in powerful, beneficial ways. Oftentimes, the writer may be unintentionally burying such feelings, and through this suggested activity students may become more open to the idea of poetry.

Have students reread "Normal Girl," one of Nina's poems in the play, as an example of how poetry can illustrate emotion. Then have students write their own emotion-based poem, using some of the writing strategies found below.

Normal girl

Normal heart

Normal brain

Then it starts

A creeping feeling: sorrow, dread

A tiny voice inside my head

Stay inside, keep out of sight

Something inside you isn't right

Venom in you, dark as night

Ugly, shameful, full of spite

Frightened girl

Jagged heart

Crooked mind

Tears you apart

Horrid girl

Broken brain

Ugly heart

Am I insane?

—Rachel Aberle, *Still • Falling*

Make a list of emotions that you noticed within the play.

- Choose one of the emotions, and, without naming it, describe it in detail, using concrete images. Think of a specific time when you may have experienced that emotion. What happened? What did it look like? Sound like? Taste like?
- How does this emotion help people?
- How does it hurt people? Or hurt you?
- Personify this emotion. If it were a person, what would they do?
- Incorporate a simile or a metaphor to further gain understanding of the emotion
  Source: archive.nwp.org/cs/public /download/nwp_file/461/Channeling _Emotion.pdf?x-r=pcfile_d

RESOURCES
WEBSITES FOR YOUTH

ANXIETY CANADA – www.anxietycanada.com

BEYOND BLUE – www.beyondblue.org.au

BREATHR APP FOR MINDFULNESS – keltymentalhealth.ca/breathr

CANADIAN MENTAL HEALTH ASSOCIATION – www.cmha.ca

DEALING WITH DEPRESSION – dwdonline.ca/

EARLY PSYCHOSIS INTERVENTION (EPI) – www.earlypsychosis.ca

FOUNDRY – www.foundrybc.ca

HEALTHY PLACE – www.healthyplace.com

HELPGUIDE.ORG – www.helpguide.org

HERE TO HELP – www.heretohelp.bc.ca

HERE TO HELP PLAINER LANGUAGE SERIES – www.heretohelp.bc.ca/plainer-language-series

JACK.ORG – jack.org

KELTY MENTAL HEALTH'S *WHERE YOU ARE* PODCAST – keltymentalhealth.ca/podcast

MINDYOURMIND – mindyourmind.ca

MINDFULNESS FOR TEENS – mindfulnessforteens.com

REACHING IN ... REACHING OUT – www.reachinginreachingout.com

REACHOUT.COM – au.reachout.com

SELF-INJURY OUTREACH AND SUPPORT – sioutreach.org

TEEN MENTAL HEALTH – teenmentalhealth.org

TEENSHEALTH – kidshealth.org/teen/your_mind/

WALK ALONG – www.walkalong.ca

YOUTH IN BC – youthinbc.com

YOUTH BEYOND BLUE – www.youthbeyondblue.com

OTHER RESOURCES

THE CANADIAN ASSOCIATION FOR SUICIDE PREVENTION SUPPORT SERVICES – suicideprevention.ca/resources/#support-services

KIDS HELP PHONE – 1-800-668-6868

If you think someone's life is in danger, call 9-1-1.

WELLNESS APPS

Available on the App Store and Google Play for free

BOOSTERBUDDY – A free app designed to help teens and young adults improve their mental health

GUIDED MIND – Relax and get guided through meditations on a variety of topics dealing with the stresses and challenges of day-to-day life

MINDSHIFT – An anxiety app developed by Anxiety Canada Association

MOOD. BY MINDYOURMIND – Co-created with youth and MindYourMind, this is an easy-to-use app that allows youth and young adults to track their moods securely on their phone

THINKFULL – For iOS devices only, aimed at older youth and young adults

WEBSITES FOR TEACHERS

CENTER FOR MENTAL HEALTH IN SCHOOLS – smhp.psych.ucla.edu

HEALTHY SCHOOLS BC – www.healthyschoolsbc.ca

KELTY MENTAL HEALTH – keltymentalhealth.ca/school-professionals

NASP (NATIONAL ASSOCIATION OF SCHOOL PSYCHOLOGISTS) – www.nasponline.org

SELF-INJURY OUTREACH AND SUPPORT FOR SCHOOL PROFESSIONALS – sioutreach.org/learn-self-injury/school-professionals/

TEEN MENTAL HEALTH FOR EDUCATORS – teenmentalhealth.org /care/educators/

PODCASTS FOR PARENTS

WHERE YOU ARE – keltymentalhealth.ca/podcast

THANK YOU!

Thank you for taking the time to use and review the *Still • Falling* Study Guide as a resource to further enrich your students' experience watching the play.

Visit our website at
www.greenthumb.bc.ca
and tell us what you thought about the play, your experience, and future play ideas. We welcome letters as well. You can also add our link to your classroom website to explore the site as an activity.

The materials contained within this study guide are provided for general information purposes only and do not constitute professional advice on the subject matter. The information provided is not intended to replace the specialized training and professional judgment of a health-care, mental-health, or school-counselling professional.

Every effort has been made to cite the owners of the copyrighted materials and to make due acknowledgment. If situations are identified where this has not been achieved, please notify Green Thumb Theatre so appropriate corrective action can be taken and appropriate credit given.

GREEN THUMB
THEATRE

THE CODE

By Rachel Aberle

STUDY
GUIDE

Supported by

Canada Council   Conseil des arts
for the Arts   du Canada

BRITISH COLUMBIA
ARTS COUNCIL
An agency of the Province of British Columbia

BRITISH
COLUMBIA
Supported by the Province of British Columbia

CITY OF
VANCOUVER

RBC | RBC Foundation
RBC Fondation

ACTUALIZE8

TABLE OF CONTENTS

The Code photos of Elizabeth Barrett, Mason Temple, and Nathan Kay by Leah Gair

Study Guide design by Markian Tarasiuk at the Art Left Design & Communications – www.theartleft.com

The materials contained within this study guide are provided for general information purposes only and do not constitute professional advice on the subject matter. The information provided is not intended to replace the specialized training and professional judgment of a health-care, mental-health, or school-counselling professional.

Every effort has been made to cite the owners of the copyrighted materials and to make due acknowledgment. If situations are identified where this has not been achieved, please notify Green Thumb Theatre so appropriate corrective action can be taken and appropriate credit given.

USING THIS GUIDE

Green Thumb Theatre is committed to telling stories that spark thought and provoke dialogue. To us, a really successful show gets people talking. The following study guide is intended to facilitate classroom discussions both before and after the performance.

In this guide we'll look deeper into understanding the themes of *The Code*. The pre- and post-show questions, activities, and discussions will invite exploration of the main topics of the show: healthy relationships, social responsibility, online bullying, and consent.

CURRICULUM CONNECTIONS

Healthy Relationships • Leadership • Social Responsibility • Self-Esteem • Personal Politics • Discrimination • Online Bullying

THE PLOT AT A GLANCE

When Moira organizes a protest at school that results in the spring dance being cancelled, students lash out at her online and in person – so she turns to her best friends Simon and Connor for support. But when Simon reveals his romantic feelings for Moira and she doesn't return them, the two fight about whether she misled him or he misinterpreted her. Feeling "friend zoned," an angry Simon goes too far and joins the barrage of online abuse of Moira with a post that ends up going viral. Stuck in the middle, Connor is forced to consider where his loyalties lie.

FULL SYNOPSIS

SCENE 1: Best friends Moira and Connor are joking around on their lunch break at school. Their other best friend, Simon, an aspiring videographer, enters while filming with a gift for Moira. Moira gets a text from the dance committee saying there has been a "dance committee crisis" and jets off. When she's gone, Simon and Connor talk about the romantic feelings Simon has developed for Moira.

SCENE 2: Moira discovers that the school has implemented a strict dress code for the spring dance, and wonders how to best address the situation, since she's in charge of planning school dances. Making matters worse, it's clear that many students think Moira came up with the new dress code, and they are now venting their feelings about her online. In an effort to try to cheer her up and assure her that the dance will still be fun, Simon suggests they go to the dance together, offering to take her for dinner and a limo ride beforehand. When Moira agrees, Simon is over the moon, and loses sight of the problem at hand. Meanwhile, Moira is still blind to Simon's actual feelings for her.

SCENE 3: Connor and Simon meet up early before school the next day, summoned by Moira, who has yet to arrive. Simon tells Connor that Moira said she'd go to the dance with him, and he starts daydreaming about his "new girlfriend." Moira arrives and reveals their task for the morning: distributing flyers to promote a school-wide walkout in protest of the new dress code. After a night of reading mean comments about her online, Moira is convinced this is the best way to make her classmates understand she is not responsible for the new rules. The three set off to distribute the posters, and we hear the speech Moira makes at the protest. She rallies support and everyone begins chanting "Our bodies, our clothes, stand up, break our code." Simon proudly films it.

SCENE 4: Immediately following the speech, Moira and Simon meet up on their way to class and talk excitedly about how well it went. The two depart to their separate classes, Moira still buzzing from the success of her speech and Simon thrilled to see his "new girlfriend" so happy.

SCENE 5: Simon and Moira meet up at lunch to celebrate the successes of the morning, but their good mood is quickly spoiled when Connor arrives and tells them that the school dance has been cancelled because of the protest. Moira's social-media platforms are quickly swarmed with hateful and hurtful comments blaming her for the cancellation. Moira believes she did the right thing by standing up for the people that the dress code affected, but she's frustrated that no one else sees it that way, not even Connor, who storms off enraged. Simon tries to cheer her up by offering other plans to replace their dance date, and quickly realizes that Moira didn't think it was a date. Hurt, Simon lashes out at Moira, who is left even more confused and upset.

SCENE 6: Before school the next day, Simon and Connor meet up and discuss a hurtful video that appeared online overnight which uses footage of Moira's speech from the protest cut together to make fun of her. Connor expresses anger at the video and concern about Moira's well-being, and he prods Simon about who he thinks might have done it. When Simon doesn't have an answer, Connor confronts him, saying that he figured out it was Simon based on the angles in the video. The two argue about whether or not Simon needs to come clean to Moira about the video's origins. Moira enters, upset about the video and a number of additional videos made by other classmates who have recut the first one. Connor leaves Simon to explain himself to Moira, and while he apologizes for the argument they had the previous day about the dance, he doesn't bring up the video. Thinking that Simon has come clean about everything, Connor re-enters and inadvertently reveals the truth to Moira. Moira demands an explanation from Simon, who brushes the video off as "just a joke" and something he did because his feelings were hurt. Moira expresses how deeply the video has hurt her, how far-reaching it has been, and how toxic and threatening the additional recut videos have become. Moira makes it clear that this has damaged their friendship beyond repair. Simon departs, realizing that his rash action has cost him his two most important friendships. Connor comforts Moira, and the two of them head in to school to face a still-angry student body together as friends.

A NOTE FROM THE PLAYWRIGHT

It feels to me that we are in the middle of a global conversation about consent. About what it is, how you define it, how one obtains it, and the intense and dire ramifications of what can happen when things happen without it. I think this is good – it's an important conversation, especially for young people to have as they begin to engage in their own relationships, romantic or otherwise.

What strikes me about the current conversation, however, is that it feels reactive. It feels like something we talk about after something bad has already happened – like a report of harassment or assault. With *The Code*, I wanted to roll that conversation back earlier in a relationship, to before anything irreversible has taken place Specifically, I wanted to look at how seemingly healthy and positive relationships can fall apart when communication breaks down.

So I wrote a show about friendship, and about what happens when people have different ideas about the nature of their friendship. Our main characters, Simon and Moira, are best friends – but Simon has been secretly hoping that they will become more. When Simon suggests that he and Moira go to the spring dance together, and she says yes, Simon is over the moon to be going on his first official date with Moira. But when it becomes clear that she thought he meant they'd go as friends, their friendship starts to break down. The two of them fight over whether she misled him or he misinterpreted her, and it becomes clear that everything he's put into their friendship, the energy and care, has been – in his mind – an investment. When he doesn't receive a return on that investment, he feels like it's all been a waste of time.

I can't tell you the number of times in my life I've heard someone complain about feeling like they've been stuck in the "friend zone." But is romance ever a fair thing to feel entitled to? How do we deal with rejection when it comes? In a situation where one person feels led on, but the other feels misinterpreted, who is right?

It's important to note that I don't think Simon is wrong to feel hurt. Handling rejection is really hard, and finding out that someone you like doesn't feel the same way about you is painful. The question is, what do we do with that pain? How do we navigate the bumps in a relationship without doing things we regret?

The questions this play prompts are tricky. There is no easy answer to any of them, but I think that's the point. It's only by having these complex and sometimes uncomfortable conversations that we can begin to move forward.

—**Rachel Aberle**

DEFINITIONS

WORDS AND PHRASES IN *THE CODE*

FRIEND ZONE: A situation in a friendship where one person has unreciprocated romantic or sexual interest for the other. Often the person who is not in the "friend zone" is unaware of the other person's romantic feelings or intentions.

DRESS CODE: A set of rules, usually written and posted, specifying the required manner of dress at a school, office, club, restaurant, etc.

CONSENT: Permission or agreement for something to happen or to do something.

RELATIONSHIP: Any time people are in relation to one another, they are in a relationship, whether that be a professional, friendly, platonic, romantic, or sexual one.

EQUALITY: The state of being equal, especially in status, rights, and opportunities.

FEMINISM: The advocacy of women's rights on the basis of the equality of the sexes. To be a feminist is to advocate those rights.

TROLLS and TROLLING: A troll is someone who posts inflammatory or inappropriate messages or comments on the internet for the purpose of upsetting other users and provoking a response – trolling.

SJW: An abbreviation for "social justice warrior," typically used in a derogatory and often sarcastic way. A person who advocates a progressive view, especially involving the treatment of racial, gender, sexual orientation, or gender-identity minorities.

WOMEN'S RIGHTS or WOMEN'S LIBERATION: Rights that promote a position of legal and social equality of women with men. A movement to combat sexual discrimination and to gain full legal, economic, vocational, educational, and social rights and opportunities for women, equal to those of men.

INTEGRITY: Adherence to moral and ethical principles, rooted in honesty.

GENDER EQUALITY: Having the same rights, status, and opportunities as others, regardless of gender.

PRE-PERFORMANCE QUESTIONS

1. What do you think is appropriate to post online? Of yourself? Of others? Is there a difference?
2. Do you ask your friends permission to post photos of them on your profile?
3. What does consent mean to you?
4. What are some major differences between friendship and romantic relationships?
5. What does a healthy relationship look like to you? How would you handle a disagreement or misunderstanding in a healthy relationship?
6. What is an appropriate way to tell someone you like them?

POST-PERFORMANCE QUESTIONS

1. Why do you think Simon kept his feelings secret from Moira?
2. Have you ever been in a situation where you've been stuck between two of your friends who are fighting? What would you have done if you were Connor?
3. If your friend had feelings for another friend, would you tell them? Why or why not?
4. What should Simon have done when his feelings were hurt?
5. Have you ever done something you regretted when you were hurt or angry?
6. Who would you reach out to if you saw something inappropriate online? Would you ever go to the police? How bad would it have to be?
7. What would someone have to do online to make you report or block them?

DISCUSSIONS AND ACTIVITIES

DISCUSSION #1: ONLINE BULLYING

What constitutes cyberbullying?

The facts of cyberbullying:

Three million kids per month are absent from school due to bullying. 20 percent of kids who are cyberbullied think about suicide, and one in ten attempt it.

The legalities of online posting:

Posting a photo of something without consent, or with intent to hurt the person captured in the image, has been a criminal offence under Canada's Criminal Code since 2015. Judges now have the authority to order the removal of intimate images from the internet if those images are posted without the consent of the person or persons in the image. However, even when the image is deleted, there may be an irreversible psychological impact on the people involved in the post.

Anyone convicted of distributing an intimate image without consent can face serious legal consequences, such as:

- imprisonment for up to five years;
- the seizure of their computer, cellphone, or other device used to share the image;
- the enforced financial reimbursement to the victim for costs they incurred removing the intimate image from the internet or elsewhere.

Discuss the ramifications of cyberbullying in class. Connect it to Simon's video in the play – one that wound up being shared much further than he anticipated. Discuss what consequences Simon may face for what he put online.

DISCUSSION #2:
FRIENDSHIP, ROMANTIC RELATIONSHIPS, AND HOW WE COMMUNICATE

Punctuation and Perception

In *The Code,* Simon takes Moira's constant texting and use of emojis to mean that she likes him. Moira sends Connor emojis as well, but somehow Simon still thinks that she is flirting with him. How does our use of specific words and punctuation change the way that a message is perceived?

Take this well-known example:

"A panda eats shoots and leaves."

vs.

"A panda eats, shoots, and leaves."

The commas in the second sentence completely change the meaning.

Questions for Discussion:

When you send texts:
• How aware are you of others' interpretations of your messages?
• Is it something you notice or think about when you text someone? Do you ever retype a text, realizing the earlier version might not make your point clear?
• Do you take responsibility for their interpretation, based on the way you communicated your message?

When you receive a text:
• How closely do you analyze the messages you receive from others?
• Have you ever sat with a friend and dissected a text to try to find its hidden meaning? What did you do if you felt like you couldn't figure it out?

ACTIVITY

Deciphering Texts

Let's look at this text conversation between Simon and Moira where they don't use punctuation. Show the three texts pictured, which say roughly the same thing, to the class.

Questions for Discussion in Groups

- What are your assumptions, based on how their messages read?
- How can use of dialogue and different phrasing lead someone to believe a person is flirting with them?
- How does the way you word something convey more than what you're actually saying (for example, tone, use of slang, grammar)?
- What is the most effective way to get your message across?

ACTIVITY

Blowing Off Steam

Part 1: A Letter from Simon to Moira

Have students write letters from Simon to Moira, or scripts for a scene between them, in which he talks to her about why he's upset.

Use these prompts to support their writing:

Imagine you're Simon – you were sure Moira felt the same way as you did. How do you feel now you know she doesn't?

What do you do with those feelings?

Is there anything Moira did that you think was unfair or unkind?

How can Simon tell Moira that she hurt him without resorting to hurting her, too?

Part 2: Alternate Ideas for Simon

Discuss an alternate situation where Simon realizes he is too hurt and angry with Moira to have a respectful conversation. What should he do? Who can he talk to?

Part 3: A Conversation between Simon and Connor

Have students write scripts for a scene between Simon and Connor in which Simon talks about why he's upset. How can Connor be a supportive friend to both Simon and Moira?

Close the activity with a group discussion about the importance of navigating disappointment and rejection in a respectful and safe manner.

DISCUSSION #3: SOCIAL CHANGE AND SCHOOL

How Much Does It Cost?

MALALA YOUSAFZAI: AN EXAMPLE OF SOCIAL CHANGE

We are never too young or too few to create social change. Take Malala Yousafzai, for example. Born in Pakistan during the Taliban occupation of the Swat district, her life was far from easy. But she believed that every child, girls as well as boys, should have a right to a free and accessible education and she advocated for that, even though she lived in a country where women don't have the same rights as they do in North America. When Malala was fourteen, she wrote a blog under a fake name, which was then featured in the *New York Times*. Though it was written under a pseudonym, this article gave a platform to her voice and the issues she was trying to resolve.

Unfortunately, life became dangerous for her after it was printed.

She was shot in the head in 2012 but survived and was later awarded the Nobel Peace Prize for her work when she was seventeen. She is still the youngest person to have been awarded one of the world's most prestigious titles. (The average age of a Nobel Peace Prize winner is sixty-two.) While Malala's story is an extreme example, that doesn't mean that each of us won't face social injustice in our own lives as well.

In *The Code*, Moira sees that her fellow female students aren't being treated fairly when a school-wide dress code is implemented, and she sees this as an opportunity to make a change in her school. When her plan backfires, she is forced to solely take the brunt of the accusations and hateful comments directed towards her.

Questions

- How far are you willing to go to stand up for what you believe in?
- How can we distinguish between when something is hard but important to do and when something is hard to do but does not fall to us? Is there anything that affects us that isn't our place to talk about?

Discuss with the class how Moira went about dealing with a dress code she found to be unfair

- What did she do that worked? What did she do that didn't work? Were her actions fair to the student body at large?
- Was she ready for the consequences of her actions? What would you do in the same situation?

These are questions with no easy or right answers. What one student may deem to be a reasonable sacrifice, another may not. Allow students a forum to dig into how they think they should go about making positive changes in their communities.

ACTIVITY

Implementing Social Change

This activity is designed to help students initiate social change in a responsible, respectful way. Be a social-change maker in your school.

What are some things you want to change in order to create a more positive school environment?

How would you change those things, and what are the roadblocks you might run into on the way?

Structure the process and decisions as outlined by the examples in this chart:

CHANGE	POSITIVES	NEGATIVES	HOW TO FIX THE NEGATIVES
Implement a "no dress code" dance at school.	Everyone can wear whatever they feel comfortable wearing.	People might use this as an opportunity to dress inappropriately or feel like they have to. The school might be worried that students may dress in a way that the administration deems disrespectful.	Have a costume-themed dance instead. Educate students about empowering themselves through self-expression.
Healthier food in the cafeteria.	Everyone will feel better and have more energy after lunch break. More people will be exposed to balanced meal options.	These options might be more expensive and therefore might deter people. How will the school get access to these options?	Talk to local politicians and get a funded community garden to grow vegetables. Have the cooking class or environmental club take care of it. Talk to local grocery stores to see if they'll donate a portion of the ingredients.

Thank you for taking the time to use and review the *The Code* Study Guide as a resource to further enrich your students' experience watching or reading the play.

Visit our website at www.greenthumb.bc.ca and tell us what you thought about the play, your experience, and future play ideas. We welcome letters as well. You can also add our link to your classroom website to explore the site as an activity.